Betty Crocker's
LOW-CALORIE
COOKING

PRENTICE HALL

New York   London   Toronto   Sydney   Tokyo   Singapore

PRENTICE HALL GENERAL REFERENCE
15 Columbus Circle
New York, New York 10023

Library of Congress Cataloging-in-Publication data

Crocker, Betty.
    [Low-calorie cooking]
    Betty Crocker's low-calorie cooking.
        p.   cm.
    Includes index.
    ISBN 0-671-84690-6
        1. Cookery. 2. Low-calorie diet. I. Title. II. Title: Low-
    calorie cooking.
    TX652.C8317 1993
    641.5′635—dc20   92-25397
                                                      CIP

Designed by Levavi & Levavi
Manufactured in the United States of America

10 9 8 7 6 5 4 3 2 1

First Edition

Cover: Hot Chicken Salad with Plum Sauce (page 34)
Back cover: Orange Roughy with Red Peppers (page 17)

Contents

Introduction

◼

Many people are interested in learning how to follow a healthful eating plan today, and BETTY CROCKER'S LOW-CALORIE COOKING provides just that. This collection of delicious, yet sensible, recipes makes losing or maintaining weight a pleasant experience. And the key to maintaining weight loss is to make healthful changes in your eating and cooking patterns. With the recipes here, you'll be able, and willing, to maintain lifelong good eating habits.

You'll find appetizers that won't use up all of your calorie allotment before dinner, including enticing recipes such as Savory Stuffed Mushrooms (25 calories) and exotic Chicken Satay (80 calories). Then move on to a satisfying collection of main dish recipes, all for 350 calories or even less. Savor Stir-fried Garlic Shrimp (230 calories), Cajun Seafood and Noodles (225 calories), Turkey with Chipotle Sauce (215 calories), Beef Stroganoff (230 calories), or Pork and Mango Salad (290 calories).

We have used reduced-calorie products—such as reduced calorie sour cream and margarine—when appropriate. In other recipes, we have used regular products and reduced the amounts to keep calories low but flavor high. If you have not cooked with reduced-calorie products, this will give you an opportunity to use them in your eating plan. Whichever recipes you choose, you'll have scrumptious, low-calorie dishes.

And we don't forget dessert! It's easy to include desserts in a sensible eating plan when you choose from Almond Apple Crisp (160 calories), Frosted Banana Bars (90 calories each) Chocolate Chip Cookies (75 calories each) or any of the other treats included here.

With BETTY CROCKER'S LOW-CALORIE COOKING, you'll find everything you need to know to start or maintain a healthful and delicious eating plan. And with Betty Crocker, you can be sure that eating right is also eating well.

THE BETTY CROCKER EDITORS

Low-Calorie Basics

We all hear about low-calorie, healthful eating, but sometimes are not quite sure what to eat to maintain our weight or achieve effective weight loss. The following pages will give you clear, straight-forward information on how to choose appropriate foods for weight loss and healthful eating, as well as a guide to the fat and cholesterol content of a useful sampling of different foods.

HOW TO USE THE NEW GOOD-EATING GUIDE

The New Good-Eating Guide (following pages) combines the recommendations of health experts within an easy-to-use chart. It defines the basic food groups and separates items within each food group to help you make the best choice for a balanced diet.

A daily diet that includes the recommended number of servings from each group contains 1200 to 1800 calories. For those who require more calories, add more servings from the four groups and the "Others" category. If you're trying to cut calories, select foods in the "Eat Anytime" category more often than those in other categories.

The number of recommended servings per day from the four food groups has changed from the first version developed by nutritionists at the U.S. Department of Agriculture. Experts now recommend eating more foods from the bread and cereals group and the fruit and vegetable group. These foods are low in fat, high in carbohydrates and often provide complex carbohydrates and fiber as well.

Many foods we eat are combinations from more than one of the food groups. For example, a casserole with meat, pasta, vegetables and cheese contains ingredients from all four groups. To apply the New Good-Eating Guide to mixed dishes, be sure the dish has more ingredients from the "Eat Anytime" and "Eat in Moderation" groups than the "Eat Occasionally" group.

THE NEW GOOD-EATING GUIDE

	BREADS/CEREALS (6 to 11 servings daily, includes whole grain, enriched breads and cereals, pasta, rice and crackers.)	FRUITS/VEGETABLES (5 to 9 servings daily. Include at least one serving citrus or other choice high in vitamin C daily. Include orange or leafy, dark green vegetables 3 to 4 times a week.)
Recommended Serving Size	1 to 1.5 ounces, ready-to-eat cereal (varies if it contains fruits, nuts) ½ cup cooked cereal, pasta or rice 1 slice bread ½ hamburger or hot dog bun ½ English muffin or bagel 1 small roll or muffin ½ pita (6 inches in diameter) 3 to 4 small or 2 large crackers 2 breadsticks (4 × ½ inch) 1 tortilla (6 inches in diameter) 3 cups popcorn 2 medium cookies	1 medium fruit such as apple, orange, banana ½ grapefruit ¾ cup juice 1 medium wedge melon ½ cup berries ¼ cup dried fruit ½ cup cooked or canned fruit or vegetable 1 medium potato 10 French-fried potatoes (2 to 3½ inches long) ½ cup raw chopped vegetables 1 cup leafy raw vegetable, such as spinach ⅛ medium avocado
Eat Anytime	Whole grain* or fortified breakfast cereal Whole grain* or enriched bread, rolls, bagels, English muffins, tortillas, low-fat crackers Brown or enriched white rice Whole grain or enriched pasta Plain popcorn, pretzels and low-fat cookies (such as fig bars) and cake (angel food)	All fresh, canned or frozen fruits and fruit juices All fresh, canned or frozen vegetables and vegetable juices Plain potato or potato with low-fat topping (such as yogurt)
Eat in Moderation	Biscuits Bread stuffing Corn bread Muffins and other quick breads Pancakes, waffles Popcorn made with added fat Taco shells	Vegetables with added butter or margarine Potatoes topped with butter, sour cream or sauces
Eat Occasionally	High-fat crackers Croissants Doughnuts Sweet rolls Snack chips (potato chips, corn chips, etc.) Most cookies and cakes	Fruit pies Deep-fried vegetables French-fried potatoes Vegetables in cream or cheese sauce
Key Nutrients Supplied	Complex carbohydrates Thiamin Iron Niacin Fiber	Vitamin A Vitamin C Fiber

*Good source of fiber.
**For those who need to limit sodium intake, these foods may be high in sodium (read nutrition labels for sodium content).

	MEAT/PROTEIN	MILK/DAIRY
	(2 to 3 servings with a total of about 6 ounces daily. Includes meat, fish, poultry and eggs. Dried beans, peas and nuts are alternatives.)	(2 servings daily: 3 for pregnant or breast-feeding women, 4 for pregnant or breast-feeding teenagers. Includes milk, yogurt, cheese, cottage cheese and pudding.)

Recommended Serving Size	2 ounces beef (maximum 3 ounces of beef daily)
	2 ounces poultry or fish
	4 ounces tofu
	Count the following as 1 ounce of meat:
	  1 egg (maximum 3 eggs weekly)
	  3 egg whites
	  2 tablespoons peanut butter or whole
	    nuts or seeds
	  ½ cup cooked beans, peas or lentils
		1 cup milk
		1 cup yogurt
		1½ ounces cheese
		1 cup pudding
		1½ cups ice cream, ice milk or frozen yogurt
		2 cups cottage cheese

Eat Anytime	*Beef:* lean beef including round, sirloin, chuck and loin *Pork:* Lean cuts including ham and tenderloin *Lamb:* Leg, arm, loin, rib *Veal:* All trimmed cuts except ground *Poultry:* All poultry without skin *Fish:* All fresh and frozen fin fish or shellfish *Other:* Egg whites, all beans, peas and lentils	Skim milk 1% low-fat milk Low-fat buttermilk** Plain nonfat or low-fat yogurt Low-fat cheeses
Eat in Moderation	*Beef:* Most cuts including all ground beef, short ribs, corned beef brisket *Pork:* Most cuts including chops, loin roast *Poultry:* All poultry with skin *Other:* Fat-free or low-fat luncheon meats,** peanut butter and other nuts or seeds *Eggs:* Limit to three eggs per week	2% low-fat milk Part-skim milk cheese** Ice milk
Eat Occasionally	*Beef:* USDA prime-grade cuts and heavily marbled cuts *Pork:* Spareribs, ground pork *Lamb:* Ground lamb *Fish:* Fried fish *Other:* Luncheon meats**, sausage**, frank-furters**, bacon**	Whole milk, cream, half-and-half Whole milk yogurt All regular cheese** such as American, Cheddar, Brie, etc. Ice cream Cream cheese and sour cream
Key Nutrients	Protein Niacin Iron Thiamin	Calcium Riboflavin Protein

*Good source of fiber.
**For those who need to limit sodium intake, these foods may be high in sodium (read nutrition labels for sodium content).

FAT AND CHOLESTEROL CONTENT OF SELECTED FOODS

FOOD	MEASURE UNIT, WEIGHT	TOTAL FAT, G	CHOLESTEROL, MG
Whole milk	1 cup	8.9	35
Skim milk	1 cup	0.4	4
Plain yogurt	6 ounces	5.5	21
Plain nonfat yogurt	6 ounces	0	5
Whipped heavy cream	2 tablespoons	1.3	4
Prepared whipped topping mix, prepared with whole milk	2 tablespoons	1.0	trace
Vanilla ice cream, 16% fat	1 cup	23.7	88
Vanilla ice milk	1 cup	5.6	18
Sour cream	1 cup	48.2	102
Lowfat sour cream	1 cup	28.8	96
Creamed cottage cheese	1 cup	9.5	31
Lowfat cottage cheese	1 cup	4.4	19
Ricotta cheese, whole milk	15 ounces	54.8	216
Lowfat ricotta cheese, skim	15 ounces	33.6	131
Cream cheese	1 ounce	9.9	31
Neufchâtel cheese	1 ounce	6.6	22
Cheddar cheese	1 ounce	9.0	30
Lowfat Cheddar cheese	1 ounce	5.0	20
Swiss cheese	1 ounce	8.0	25
Lowfat Swiss cheese	1 ounce	5.0	20
Lard	1 tablespoon	12.8	12
Butter	1 tablespoon	11.5	31
Margarine, corn	1 tablespoon	11.5	0
Reduced-calorie margarine	1 tablespoon	8.0	0
Eggs	1 large	5.1	217
Cholesterol-free egg product	¼ cup	0	0
Vegetable oil, corn	1 tablespoon	13.6	0
Nonstick cooking spray	1 spray	1.0	0
Mayonnaise, soybean	1 tablespoon	11.0	8
Cholesterol-free reduced-calorie mayonnaise	1 tablespoon	5.0	0
Italian salad dressing	1 tablespoon, bottled	8.0	0
Reduced-calorie Italian salad dressing	1 tablespoon, bottled	0	0
Blue cheese salad dressing	1 tablespoon, bottled	6.0	0
Reduced-calorie blue cheese salad dressing	1 tablespoon, bottled	2.0	0
Egg noodles	2 ounces, dry	3.0	70
Cholesterol-free noodles	2 ounces, dry	1.0	0
Tuna, oil packed, drained	3 ounces, canned	6.9	26
Tuna, water packed, drained	3 ounces, canned	2.1	35
Salmon, Chinook	3 ounces, baked	11.0	69
Flounder, sole	3 ounces, baked	1.3	58
Crab legs	3 ounces, cooked	1.0	45
Imitation crabmeat sticks	3 ounces, cooked	1.1	17
Ground beef	3 ounces, broiled	17.6	76
Extra-lean ground beef	3 ounces, broiled	13.9	71
Beef boneless rib roast	3 ounces, roasted	8.0	65
Beef top round steak	3 ounces, broilied	6.0	72
Pork shoulder blade steak	3 ounces, braised	14.0	83
Pork loin tenderloin	3 ounces, roasted	4.0	79
Chicken, dark meat without skin	3 ounces, roasted	8.3	79
Chicken, light meat without skin	3 ounces, roasted	3.8	72
Turkey, dark meat without skin	3 ounces, roasted	6.1	72
Turkey, white meat without skin	3 ounces, roasted	2.7	59
White layer cake with white frosting	½ slice	14.0	0
White angel food cake, unfrosted	½ slice	0	0

Sources: Compiled by General Mills, Inc. from U.S. Department of Agriculture Handbook #8, Michigan State University data base, Egg Board, product labels and manufacturer information.

1983 METROPOLITAN HEIGHT AND WEIGHT TABLES

Below are height and weight tables for men and women that serve as a guide to establishing a comfortable weight.

WOMEN				MEN			
Height	Small Frame	Medium Frame	Large Frame	Height	Small Frame	Medium Frame	Large Frame
4'10"	102–111	109–121	118–131	5'2"	128–134	131–141	138–150
4'11"	103–113	111–123	120–134	5'3"	130–136	133–143	140–153
5'0"	104–115	113–126	122–137	5'4"	132–138	135–145	142–156
5'1"	106–118	115–129	125–140	5'5"	134–140	137–148	144–160
5'2"	108–121	118–132	128–143	5'6"	136–142	139–151	146–164
5'3"	111–124	121–135	131–147	5'7"	138–145	142–154	149–168
5'4"	114–127	124–138	134–151	5'8"	140–148	145–157	152–172
5'5"	117–130	127–141	137–155	5'9"	142–151	148–160	155–176
5'6"	120–133	130–144	140–159	5'10"	144–154	151–163	158–180
5'7"	123–136	133–147	143–163	5'11"	146–157	154–166	161–184
5'8"	126–139	136–150	146–167	6'0"	149–160	157–170	164–188
5'9"	129–142	139–153	149–170	6'1"	152–164	160–174	168–192
5'10"	132–145	142–156	152–173	6'2"	155–168	164–178	172–197
5'11"	135–148	145–159	155–176	6'3"	158–172	167–182	176–202
6'0"	138–151	148–162	158–179	6'4"	162–176	171–187	181–207

Note: Weights at ages 25 to 59 based on lowest mortality. Weight in pounds according to frame (in indoor clothing weighing 3 pounds, shoes with 1-inch heels).
Source: Courtesy of Metropolitan Life Insurance Company Statistical Bulletin.

Note‹ Weights at ages 25 to 59 based on lowest mortality. Weight in pounds according to frame (in indoor clothing weighing 5 pounds, shoes with 1-inch heels.)
Source: Courtesy of Metropolitan Life Insurance Company Statistical Bulletin.

HOW TO USE NUTRITION INFORMATION

Nutrition Information Per Serving for each recipe includes the amounts of calories, protein, carbohydrate, fat, cholesterol and sodium.

• If ingredient choices are given, the first listed ingredient is used in recipe nutrition information calculations.

• When ingredient ranges or more than one serving size is indicated, the first weight or serving is used to calculate nutrition information.

• "If desired" ingredients and recipe variations are not included in nutrition information calculations.

Guidelines for daily nutrient needs of healthy adults are listed below.

Calories:	2000
Fat:	no more than 67 grams
Cholesterol:	300 mg or less
Sodium:	2200 mg

Health experts recommend no more than 30% of daily calories come from fat. Use the following example to determine the percentage of daily calories from fat.

?? Fat Grams × 9 Calories per Fat Gram ÷ ?? Total Calories × 100 = % Calories From Fat

MENUS

Dinner for a Hot Day
Fresh Tomato Salsa (page 7) with cut-up Fresh
   Vegetables
Cold Poached Salmon with Green
   Sauce (page 24)
Dinner Rolls
Tossed Green Salad
Watermelon with Blackberries and Pear
   Puree (page 71)

Company Dinner
Chicken Terrine with Crackers (page 11)
Scallops with Red Pepper Sauce (page 26)
Hot Noodles
Steamed Asparagus
Blueberry-Lime Torte (page 75)

Quick Supper
Vegetable Beef Burgers (page 61) served with
   Pita Bread
Brownies (page 82)

Family Dinner
Pita Pizza Bites (page 9)
Herbed Chicken (page 38)
Baked Potatoes
Green Beans with Almonds
Almond-Apple Crisp (page 76)

International Dinner
Melon and Prosciutto (page 8)
Pork and Broccoli Risotto (page 64)
Chocolate Swirl Cheesecake (page 83)

Cozy Dinner for a Cold Night
Savory Stuffed Mushrooms (page 2)
Beef Stroganoff with Hot Egg Noodles (page 58)
Steamed Broccoli
Rice Pudding (page 82)

1

Ample Appetizers

Dilled Vegetables

½ medium head cauliflower (about
  1 pound), separated into flowerets
½ pound green beans
1 small red onion, sliced and separated
  into rings
½ cup low-calorie Italian dressing
1 teaspoon dried dill weed
½ teaspoon crushed red pepper

Heat 1 inch salted water (¼ teaspoon salt to 1 cup water) to boiling. Add cauliflower and green beans. Cover and heat to boiling; reduce heat. Boil 6 to 8 minutes or until crisp-tender; drain.

Place cauliflower, beans and onion in shallow glass dish. Shake remaining ingredients in tightly covered container; pour over vegetables. Cover and refrigerate at least 4 hours, stirring once, to blend flavors; drain. **8 servings**

PER SERVING: Calories 45; Protein 2 g; Carbohydrate 7 g; Fat 2 g; Cholesterol 0 mg; Sodium 130 mg

Snappy Stuffed Tomatillos

These tangy fruits grow in papery husks that are easily peeled away, revealing the bright green, sticky skins. Tomatillos keep in the refrigerator as long as 2 or 3 weeks, so you can stock up on them.

20 tomatillos or cherry tomatoes (1¼ to
  1½ inches in diameter)
⅔ cup shredded Cheddar cheese
½ cup whole kernel corn
2 packages (3 ounces each) cream
  cheese, softened
2 green onions (with tops), sliced
1 teaspoon ground red chilies
Ground red chilies

Cut thin slice from stem ends of tomatillos. Remove pulp and seeds with melon baller or spoon. Mix Cheddar cheese, corn, cream cheese, onions and 1 teaspoon ground red chilies. Fill tomatillos with cheese mixture. Sprinkle with ground red chilies. Cover and refrigerate until serving time. Garnish with cilantro and green onions if desired. **20 appetizers**

PER TOMATILLO: Calories 55; Protein 2 g; Carbohydrate 2 g; Fat 4 g; Cholesterol 15 mg; Sodium 55 mg

Savory Stuffed Mushrooms

Serve 6 of these with slices of ripe tomato for a fresh, summertime lunch or dinner.

36 medium mushrooms (about 1 pound)
¼ cup chopped onion (about 1 small)
¼ cup chopped green bell pepper
2 tablespoons reduced-calorie margarine
1½ cups soft bread crumbs
½ teaspoon salt
½ teaspoon dried thyme leaves
¼ teaspoon ground turmeric
¼ teaspoon pepper

Remove stems from mushrooms; reserve caps. Finely chop enough stems to measure ⅓ cup. Cook and stir chopped mushroom stems, onion and bell pepper in margarine until tender, about 5 minutes; remove from heat. Stir in remaining ingredients.

Heat oven to 350°. Fill reserved mushroom caps with stuffing mixture; place mushrooms, filled sides up, in baking or broiler pan sprayed with nonstick cooking spray. Bake uncovered 15 minutes.

Set oven control to broil. Broil with tops 3 to 4 inches from heat until light brown, about 2 minutes. Serve hot.   **36 appetizers**

PER APPETIZER: Calories 25; Protein 1 g; Carbohydrate 4 g; Fat 1 g; Cholesterol 0 mg; Sodium 70 mg

---

MICROWAVE DIRECTIONS: Place chopped mushroom stems, onion, bell pepper and margarine in 1-quart microwavable casserole. Cover tightly and microwave on high 1 minute; stir. Cover tightly and microwave until tender, 1 to 2 minutes longer. Continue as directed. Arrange mushroom caps, filled sides up (smallest mushrooms in center), on two 10-inch microwavable plates. Microwave 1 plate at a time uncovered on high 1 minute; rotate plate ½ turn. Microwave until hot, 30 to 60 seconds longer.

What Is a Calorie?

A calorie measures energy, specifically the energy produced when food is broken down by the body. Different foods provide the key nutrients we need—protein, carbohydrates and fat—and supply the body with energy in the form of calories.

To maintain a certain weight, a person should eat roughly the same number of calories as he or she expends in daily activity. If you decrease your level of activity while eating the same number of calories, it's easy to gain weight. The good news is that, conversely, if you eat the same amount of food and raise your activity level through regular exercise, weight loss is sure to follow.

Smoky Mushroom Spread

This is a versatile spread—you'll love it with crackers, vegetables or as an accompaniment to meats or fish.

3 cups finely chopped mushrooms (about 8 ounces)
½ cup finely chopped onion (about 1 medium)
1 clove garlic, finely chopped
1 tablespoon all-purpose flour
¼ teaspoon salt
⅛ teaspoon pepper
1 teaspoon Worcestershire sauce
¼ teaspoon liquid smoke
½ package (8-ounce size) Neufchâtel cheese, cut into cubes
½ cup nonfat plain yogurt
1 slice bacon, crisply cooked and finely crumbled

Spray 10-inch nonstick skillet with nonstick cooking spray; heat over medium heat until hot. Cook mushrooms, onion and garlic until onion is tender, about 2 minutes. Stir in flour, salt and pepper thoroughly. Stir in remaining ingredients except bacon. Heat until hot; sprinkle with bacon. Serve hot or cold with melba toast rounds if desired. **about 1½ cups spread**

PER TABLESPOON: Calories 2; Protein 1 g; Carbohydrate 2 g; Fat 1 g; Cholesterol 4 mg; Sodium 50 mg

Dilled Cucumber-Shrimp Spread

1 cup dry curd low-fat cottage cheese
½ package (8-ounce size) Neufchâtel cheese, softened
¼ cup nonfat plain yogurt
1 tablespoon snipped fresh or 1 teaspoon dried dill weed
1 teaspoon lemon juice
Freshly ground pepper
1 cup well-drained shredded seeded cucumber (about 1 medium)
1 can (4½ ounces) small shrimp, rinsed and drained

Place all ingredients except pepper, cucumber and shrimp in workbowl of food processor fitted with steel blade or in blender container. Cover and process or blend until smooth, about 30 seconds. Spread mixture in shallow 9-inch serving plate; sprinkle with pepper. Top with cucumber and shrimp. Cover and refrigerate at least 2 hours. Serve with vegetable slices or crackers if desired. **about 2¼ cups spread**

PER TABLESPOON: Calories 15; Protein 2 g; Carbohydrate 0 g; Fat 1 g; Cholesterol 5 mg; Sodium 20 mg

Herbed Yogurt Cheese

Homemade yogurt cheese, with half the calories of rich cream cheese, has the same smooth texture. It is delicious and versatile even without the dill weed and garlic. You can pack the cheese into a heart-shaped coeur à la crème *mold rather than a strainer. Because these molds have fewer drainage holes, refrigerate the cheese for 6 hours longer.*

4 cups nonfat plain yogurt
¼ cup snipped fresh or 1 tablespoon dried dill weed
1 teaspoon salt
2 cloves garlic, finely chopped

Line 6-inch strainer with coffee filter or double thickness cheesecloth. Place strainer over bowl. Mix all ingredients; pour into strainer. Cover strainer and bowl; refrigerate at least 12 hours. Unmold onto plate. Garnish with freshly ground pepper and additional dill weed if desired.

about 1¼ cups cheese spread

PER TABLESPOON: Calories 25; Protein 2 g; Carbohydrate 3 g; Fat 0 g; Cholesterol 0 mg; Sodium 140 mg

Eggplant Dip

For an extra flavor boost, stir in a few tablespoons of plain yogurt or sesame-seed paste.

1 small eggplant (about 1 pound)
1 small onion, cut into fourths
1 clove garlic
¼ cup lemon juice
1 tablespoon olive or vegetable oil
1 teaspoon salt
Assorted raw vegetables

Heat oven to 400°. Prick eggplant 3 or 4 times with fork. Bake about 40 minutes or until tender; cool. Pare eggplant; cut into cubes. Place eggplant, onion, garlic, lemon juice, oil and salt in blender. Cover and blend on high speed until smooth. Serve with vegetables.

about 2 cups dip

PER TABLESPOON: Calories 10; Protein 0 g; Carbohydrate 1 g; Fat 0 g; Cholesterol 0 mg; Sodium 70 mg

Mustard Dip

Try low-fat sour cream for even fewer calories!

½ **cup sour cream**
½ **cup plain yogurt**
1 **tablespoon finely chopped fresh parsley**
1 **teaspoon onion powder**
½ **teaspoon garlic salt**
1 **tablespoon Dijon mustard**

Mix all ingredients. Cover and refrigerate at least 1 hour. Serve with meatballs, cocktail sausages or fresh vegetables if desired.

about 1 cup dip

PER TABLESPOON: Calories 20; Protein 1 g; Carbohydrate 1 g; Fat 2 g; Cholesterol 5 mg; Sodium 90 mg

Fruit Kabobs with Pineapple Dip

This recipe makes enough dip to serve on more than one occasion. Pineapple and cheese is a classic combination, served here with little fruit skewers—wonderful party food.

Pineapple Dip (below)
30 **seedless green grapes**
30 **pineapple chunks, about ¾ inch each (¼ pineapple) or 1 can (8¼ ounces) sliced pineapple in juice, drained and each slice cut into eighths**
30 **mandarin orange segments or 1 can (11 ounces) mandarin orange segments, drained**
15 **strawberries, cut in half**

Prepare Pineapple Dip. Place any combination of 4 pieces of fruit on plastic or wooden picks. Serve with Pineapple Dip.

about 30 appetizers

PER APPETIZER: Calories 10; Protein 0 g; Carbohydrate 3 g; Fat 0 g; Cholesterol 0 mg; Sodium 1 mg

Pineapple Dip

1 **package (8 ounces) Neufchâtel cheese, softened**
1 **cup nonfat plain yogurt**
2 **tablespoons honey**
2 **teaspoons crushed gingerroot**
1 **can (8¼ ounces) crushed pineapple in juice, drained**

Beat cheese, yogurt, honey and gingerroot until creamy. Fold in pineapple; cover and refrigerate at least 1 hour. **about 3 cups dip**

PER TABLESPOON: Calories 20; Protein 1 g; Carbohydrate 2 g; Fat 1 g; Cholesterol 5 mg; Sodium 25 mg

Green Herb Dip

Green Herb Dip

¾ **cup plain low-fat yogurt**
¼ **cup cholesterol-free reduced-calorie mayonnaise or salad dressing**
¼ **teaspoon salt**
½ **cup watercress leaves**
½ **cup fresh parsley leaves**
¼ **cup fresh basil leaves**
1 green onion (with top), cut into 1-inch pieces

Place yogurt, mayonnaise and salt in blender or food processor. Add remaining ingredients. Cover and blend or process about 30 seconds, stopping blender occasionally to scrape sides, until finely chopped. Cover and refrigerate about 1 hour or until slightly thickened and chilled. Serve with raw vegetables if desired.

about 1 cup dip

PER TABLESPOON: Calories 20; Protein 1 g; Carbohydrate 1 g; Fat 1 g; Cholesterol 0 mg; Sodium 75 mg

Fresh Tomato Salsa

This fresh, piquant tomato-based sauce adds excitement to everything it touches— taco chips, fish, eggs, meat. When you make Fresh Tomato Salsa, you also have a delicious dip that's low in calories.

3 medium tomatoes, seeded and chopped (about 3 cups)
½ **cup sliced green onions (with tops)**
½ **cup chopped green bell pepper**
2 to 3 tablespoons lime juice
2 tablespoons chopped fresh cilantro
1 tablespoon finely chopped jalapeño chilies
½ **teaspoon salt**
3 cloves garlic, finely chopped

Mix all ingredients. Serve with tortilla chips, crackers or vegetables if desired.

about 3½ cups

PER TABLESPOON: Calories 2; Protein 0 g; Carbohydrate 1 g; Fat 0 g; Cholesterol 0 mg; Sodium 10 mg

Coping While Counting Calories

Most people find they have some trouble spots when trying to change eating habits. Below are tips to help you create healthful eating patterns.

- Nibbling on leftovers? Cover them and put them away as soon as you finish your meal. Or give them away. Throw them out, if you must. Serve portions that seem skimpy on luncheon, not dinner, plates.
- Impulsive eating? Stick to a planned daily menu that "schedules" snacks. Before eating any "unplanned" food, drink a glass of water and make yourself wait ten minutes. Don't skip meals. Shop only from lists you've made out at home. Keep food out of sight. If someone is snacking and you are tempted, leave the room.
- Late-night snacking? Save your "scheduled" snacks until the evening comes around.
- Mindlessly snacking while watching television (or reading, or studying)? Limit your eating to one location, the dining room table, for example. Make it a rule not to munch while doing something else. If you don't think you can watch TV without eating, then turn off the television and do something else.

Melon and Prosciutto

Prosciutto is a type of Italian ham cured by a special drying process, usually sold very thinly sliced. For even more flavor, sprinkle the melon with fresh lemon or lime juice before wrapping it with prosciutto.

1 large cantaloupe, casaba, honeydew or Spanish melon (about 3 pounds)
¼ pound thinly sliced prosciutto, cut into 1-inch strips*

Cut melon in half. Scoop out seeds and fibers. Cut each half lengthwise into 6 wedges and remove rind. Cut crosswise slits 1½ inches apart in each melon wedge. Place several strips of prosciutto over each wedge. Push prosciutto into slits using blade of table knife.

12 servings

PER SERVING: Calories 25; Protein 2 g; Carbohydrate 3 g; Fat 1 g; Cholesterol 2 mg; Sodium 110 mg

MELON AND PROSCIUTTO BITES: Cut each melon wedge into 6 pieces. Wrap each piece in strips of prosciutto. Secure with wooden picks.

72 appetizers

¼ pound thinly sliced ham can be substituted for the prosciutto.

Pita Pizza Bites

2 pita breads (6-inch diameter)
2 cups sliced mushrooms (about
   5 ounces)*
1 small red onion, thinly sliced
¼ cup chopped green bell pepper
2 tablespoons chopped fresh or 2 teaspoons dried basil leaves
1 cup finely shredded mozzarella cheese
   (4 ounces)
1 tablespoon grated Parmesan cheese

Heat oven to 425°. Split each bread in half around edge with knife to make 4 rounds. Place rounds, cut sides up, on ungreased cookie sheet. Place mushrooms on bread rounds. Top with onion and bell pepper. Sprinkle with basil and cheeses. Bake 8 to 10 minutes or until cheese is melted. Cut each round into 8 pieces. **32 appetizers**

PER APPETIZER: Calories 25; Protein 1 g; Carbohydrate 3 g; Fat 1 g; Cholesterol 2 mg; Sodium 40 mg

---

* 1 can (4 ounces) mushroom stems and pieces, drained, can be substituted for fresh mushrooms.

Potato Snacks

Here is the wonderful flavor of French-fried potatoes without all that fat. These homemade chips recall the famous Saratoga chips of days gone by.

3 medium unpared potatoes (about
   1 pound)
Vegetable oil
1 teaspoon salt
½ teaspoon sugar
½ teaspoon paprika
¼ teaspoon dry mustard
⅛ teaspoon garlic powder

Set oven control to broil. Cut potatoes lengthwise into eighths. Place potatoes, cut sides down, in ungreased jelly roll pan, 15½ × 10½ × 1 inch. Brush lightly with oil. Mix remaining ingredients; sprinkle potatoes with half of the mixture. Broil potatoes with tops about 3 inches from heat until they bubble slightly, about 10 minutes. Turn; brush with oil and sprinkle with remaining salt mixture. Broil until golden brown and tender, about 5 minutes longer. Serve with reduced-calorie sour cream if desired.

6 servings, 4 pieces each

PER SERVING: Calories 80; Protein 2 g; Carbohydrate 14 g; Fat 2 g; Cholesterol 0 mg; Sodium 370 mg

---

Chicken Terrine

Chicken Terrine

Serve thinly sliced with crackers.

¼ **cup chopped fresh parsley**
1½ **pounds boneless skinless chicken breasts**
2 **tablespoons chopped shallots**
1 **tablespoon chopped fresh or 1 teaspoon dried thyme leaves**
1 **tablespoon vegetable oil**
1 **teaspoon salt**
2 **egg whites**
½ **cup chopped red bell pepper (about 1 small)**

Heat oven to 350°. Line loaf pan, 8½ × 4½ × 2½ inches, with aluminum foil. Sprinkle parsley in bottom of pan. Trim fat from chicken breasts. Cut chicken into 1-inch pieces. Place chicken in food processor. Cover and process until coarsely ground. Add remaining ingredients except bell pepper. Cover and process until smooth. Stir in bell pepper.

Spread in pan. Cover tightly with foil. Bake 1 hour; remove foil cover. Bake 20 to 30 minutes longer or until meat thermometer inserted in center registers 180°. Cover and let stand 1 hour. Refrigerate at least 3 hours. Invert onto serving platter. Remove pan and foil.   **16 servings**

PER SERVING: Calories 65; Protein 10 g; Carbohydrate 1 g; Fat 2 g; Cholesterol 30 mg; Sodium 175 mg

Chicken Satay

An authentic Asian satay consists of marinated meat or seafood grilled on skewers and served with a sauce. Hoisin and plum sauce replace the high-fat peanut sauce that usually accompanies satay. If using bamboo skewers, soak skewers in water at least 30 minutes before using to prevent burning.

1 **pound boneless skinless chicken breasts**
⅓ **cup hoisin sauce**
⅓ **cup plum sauce**
2 **tablespoons sliced green onions (with tops)**
1 **tablespoon grated gingerroot**
2 **tablespoons dry sherry or chicken broth**
2 **tablespoons white vinegar**

Trim fat from chicken breasts. Cut chicken lengthwise into ½-inch strips. Mix all ingredients except chicken in large glass or plastic bowl. Add chicken; toss to coat. Cover and refrigerate 2 hours.

Set oven control to broil. Remove chicken from marinade; drain. Reserve marinade. Thread 2 pieces chicken on each of twelve 10-inch skewers. Place on rack in broiler pan. Broil with tops 3 to 4 inches from heat about 8 minutes, turning once, until done. Heat marinade to boiling in 1-quart saucepan. Serve with chicken.

12 appetizers

PER APPETIZER: Calories 80; Protein 8 g; Carbohydrate 7 g; Fat 2 g; Cholesterol 25 mg; Sodium 85 mg

Savory Fish en Papillote

2
Fish and Shellfish

Savory Fish en Papillote

Cooking fish in parchment paper keeps it moist—without added calories!

1 pound orange roughy or other lean fish
  fillets
4 twelve-inch circles cooking parchment
  paper
4 teaspoons chopped fresh or 1 teaspoon dried oregano
¼ teaspoon salt
⅛ teaspoon pepper
1 small onion, thinly sliced
1 small tomato, thinly sliced
1 small zucchini, thinly sliced
¼ cup sliced ripe olives

Heat oven to 400°. Cut fish fillets into 4 serving pieces. Place each piece fish on half of each parchment circle. Sprinkle fish with oregano, salt and pepper. Layer onion, tomato, zucchini and olives on fish. Fold other half of circle over fish and vegetables. Beginning at one end, seal edge by turning up and folding tightly 2 or 3 times. Twist each end several times to secure. Place on ungreased cookie sheet.

Bake 20 to 25 minutes or until vegetables are crisp-tender and fish flakes easily with fork. To serve, cut a large X in top of each packet; fold back points. **4 servings**

PER SERVING: Calories 160; Protein 25 g; Carbohydrate 5 g; Fat 4 g; Cholesterol 35 mg; Sodium 260 mg

MICROWAVE DIRECTIONS: Prepare and wrap fish fillets and vegetables as directed. Arrange packets in circle in microwave oven. Microwave on high 7 to 8 minutes, rearranging packets after 4 minutes, until vegetables are crisp-tender and fish flakes easily with fork. Let stand 3 minutes before cutting X in packets.

Mustard-topped Fish

4 small halibut steaks, 1 inch thick
1/8 teaspoon pepper
2 tablespoons margarine or butter,
   melted
2 egg whites
1/4 cup grated Parmesan cheese
2 tablespoons Dijon mustard
2 tablespoons chopped green onions
   (with tops)

Sprinkle fish steaks with pepper. Place fish on rack in broiler pan; brush with 1 tablespoon of the margarine. Set oven control to broil. Broil fish with tops 2 to 3 inches from heat until light brown, about 5 minutes. Turn; brush with remaining margarine. Broil until fish flakes easily with fork, 5 to 8 minutes.

Beat egg whites until stiff but not dry. Fold in cheese, mustard and onions. Spread mixture over fish. Broil until tops are golden brown, about 1 1/2 minutes. **4 servings**

PER SERVING: Calories 205; Protein 30 g; Carbohydrate 1 g; Fat 9 g; Cholesterol 80 mg; Sodium 400 mg

Chili Skillet Fish

1 pound fish fillets
1 medium onion, thinly sliced
2 tablespoons olive or vegetable oil
1/2 teaspoon salt
1/4 teaspoon coarsely ground pepper
1 can (4 ounces) chopped green chilies,
   drained
10 pimiento-stuffed green olives
1/4 cup dry white wine
1 tablespoon lemon juice
Lemon wedges

If fish fillets are large, cut into 4 serving pieces. Place onion in oil in 10-inch skillet. Place fish on onion; sprinkle with salt and pepper. Spoon chilies onto fish; top with olives. Mix wine and lemon juice; pour over fish. Heat to boiling; reduce heat. Cover and simmer until fish flakes easily with fork, about 10 minutes. Serve with lemon wedges. **4 servings**

PER SERVING: Calories 180; Protein 20 g; Carbohydrate 5 g; Fat 9 g; Cholesterol 55 mg; Sodium 920 mg

Steamed Fish with Ginger

Steaming is a wonderful, low-calorie method of cooking.

1 whole pike or sea bass (2 pounds)
2 tablespoons lemon juice
1 tablespoon vegetable oil
1 teaspoon salt
2 teaspoons finely chopped gingerroot
2 green onions
Ginger Sauce (right)

Remove head from fish. Slash fish crosswise 3 times on each side. Mix lemon juice, oil, salt and gingerroot; rub in cavity and on outside of fish. Cover and refrigerate 1 hour.

Place fish on rack over water in steamer or roaster (water should not touch bottom of rack; if necessary, elevate rack by placing on custard cups). Cover tightly and heat to boiling; reduce heat. Steam over boiling water until fish flakes easily with fork, about 20 minutes. (Add boiling water if necessary.)

Cut green onions into 2-inch pieces; cut pieces into thin strips. Prepare Ginger Sauce. Carefully remove skin from fish; place fish on serving platter. Pour half of the Ginger Sauce over fish; sprinkle with green onions. Serve with remaining Ginger Sauce.   **6 servings**

PER SERVING: Calories 215; Protein 27 g; Carbohydrate 6 g; Fat 9 g; Cholesterol 75 mg; Sodium 1280 mg

Ginger Sauce

1 tablespoon finely chopped gingerroot
1 teaspoon finely chopped garlic
2 tablespoons vegetable oil
½ cup dry white wine
¼ cup soy sauce
¼ cup chili sauce
½ teaspoon sugar
4 to 6 drops red pepper sauce
1 teaspoon cornstarch
2 tablespoons cold water

Cook and stir gingerroot and garlic in oil in 1-quart saucepan until light brown. Stir in wine, soy sauce, chili sauce, sugar and pepper sauce. Heat to boiling; reduce heat. Cover and simmer 10 minutes. Mix cornstarch and cold water; stir into ginger mixture. Heat to boiling; boil and stir 1 minute.

Tips for Low-Calorie Cooking

- Use nonstick cookware and nonstick cooking spray to lessen the amount of fat used in cooking.
- Baste meats with their own juices, broth or vegetable juices, rather than with margarine or butter.
- Use low-fat, nonfat or skim milk products when cooking. There are many new milk products lower in fat available today, including cheeses and yogurts.
- Use strongly flavored ingredients in salad dressings and reduce or omit the amount of oil used.
- Broil, bake, roast, grill, steam and microwave food when possible, to cut down on fat. When stir-frying, use a small amount of oil, just enough to coat the pan or wok.

Vegetable-stuffed Sole

½ teaspoon salt
½ teaspoon chopped fresh or ½ teaspoon dried dill weed
¼ teaspoon pepper
6 sole or other lean fish fillets (about 2 pounds)
2 medium carrots, cut into julienne strips
1 green bell pepper, cut into julienne strips
¼ cup dry white wine or apple juice
2 tablespoons margarine or butter
2 tablespoons all-purpose flour
½ teaspoon salt
⅛ teaspoon pepper
1 cup milk
¼ cup dry white wine or apple juice

Heat oven to 350°. Mix ½ teaspoon salt, the dill weed and ¼ teaspoon pepper. Sprinkle over fish fillets. Divide carrot and bell pepper strips among fish. Roll up fish and place, seam sides down, in ungreased rectangular baking dish, 13 × 9 × 2 inches. Pour ¼ cup wine over fish. Cover with aluminum foil and bake about 40 minutes or until fish flakes easily with fork.

Heat margarine in 1½-quart saucepan until melted. Stir in flour, ½ teaspoon salt and ⅛ teaspoon pepper. Cook over medium heat, stirring constantly, until smooth and bubbly; remove from heat. Stir in milk and ¼ cup wine. Heat to boiling, stirring constantly. Boil and stir 1 minute.

Arrange fish on serving platter. Pour sauce over fish. Garnish with dill weed if desired.

6 servings

PER SERVING: Calories 225; Protein 28 g; Carbohydrate 10 g; Fat 6 g; Cholesterol 45 mg; Sodium 440 mg

MICROWAVE DIRECTIONS: Place carrot strips in rectangular microwavable dish, 11 × 7 × 1½ inches. Add 1 tablespoon wine. Cover tightly and microwave on high about 4 minutes or until crisp-tender. Remove with slotted spoon. Prepare fish fillets as directed. Arrange seam sides down around sides of dish. Drizzle with 3 tablespoons wine. Cover tightly and microwave on high 10 to 12 minutes, rotating dish ½ turn after 5 minutes, until fish flakes easily with fork. Let stand covered 3 minutes. Remove to warm platter and keep warm.

Microwave margarine in 4-cup microwavable measure uncovered on high 15 to 30 seconds or until melted. Stir in flour, ½ teaspoon salt and ⅛ teaspoon pepper. Gradually stir in milk and ¼ cup wine. Microwave uncovered on high about 4 minutes, stirring every minute, until thickened.

Cod with Marinated Tomatoes

Tomatoes add zest and color to this tasty dish.

2 medium tomatoes, chopped (about 1½ cups)
¼ cup sliced green onions (with tops)
2 tablespoons vinegar
2 tablespoons water
1 tablespoon capers
½ teaspoon salt
¼ teaspoon red pepper sauce
1 pound cod fillets

Mix tomatoes, onions, vinegar, water, capers, salt and pepper sauce in glass jar or bowl. Cover and let stand at room temperature at least 4 hours.

If fish fillets are large, cut into 4 serving pieces. Heat 1½ inches water to boiling in 10-inch skillet; reduce heat. Place fish in single layer in skillet. Heat to boiling; reduce heat. Simmer uncovered until fish flakes easily with fork, 4 to 6 minutes. Remove fish with slotted spoon. Drain tomato mixture; spoon over fish. **4 servings**

PER SERVING: Calories 105; Protein 20 g; Carbohydrate 4 g; Fat 1 g; Cholesterol 55 mg; Sodium 360 mg

MICROWAVE DIRECTIONS: Prepare tomato mixture as directed. Arrange fish with thickest parts to outside edges in ungreased square microwavable dish, 8 × 8 × 2 inches. Cover tightly and microwave on high 3 minutes; rotate dish ½ turn. Microwave until fish flakes easily with fork, 2 to 4 minutes longer. Remove fish with slotted spoon. Drain tomato mixture; spoon over fish.

Orange Roughy with Red Peppers

For extra-crisp peppers when cooking this dish in the microwave, omit the step of cooking the peppers before adding the fish.

1 pound orange roughy or lean fish fillets
1 teaspoon olive or vegetable oil
1 small onion, cut into thin slices
2 red or green bell peppers, cut into julienne strips
1 tablespoon snipped fresh or 1 teaspoon dried thyme leaves
¼ teaspoon pepper

If fish fillets are large, cut into 4 servings pieces. Heat oil in 10-inch nonstick skillet. Layer onion and bell peppers in skillet; sprinkle with half of the thyme and half of the pepper. Place fish over bell peppers and sprinkle with remaining thyme and pepper.

Cover and cook over low heat 15 minutes. Uncover and cook until fish flakes easily with fork, 10 to 15 minutes longer. **4 servings**

PER SERVING: Calories 145; Protein 20 g; Carbohydrate 6 g; Fat 5 g; Cholesterol 110 mg; Sodium 35 mg

MICROWAVE DIRECTIONS: Omit oil. Layer onion and bell peppers in rectangular microwavable dish, 12 × 7½ × 2 inches; sprinkle with half of the thyme and half of the pepper. Cover with vented plastic wrap and microwave on high 2 minutes. Arrange fish, thickest parts to outside edges, on bell peppers; sprinkle with remaining thyme and pepper. Cover with vented plastic wrap and microwave 4 minutes; rotate dish ½ turn. Microwave until fish flakes easily with fork, 3 to 5 minutes longer. Let stand covered 3 minutes.

Oven-poached Halibut

Oven-poached Halibut

Serve with cocktail sauce or Green Sauce (page 24).

4 halibut steaks, 1 inch thick (about
   1½ pounds)
¼ teaspoon salt
4 sprigs dill weed
4 slices lemon
5 black peppercorns
¼ cup dry white wine or water

Heat oven to 450°. Place fish steaks in ungreased rectangular baking dish, 12 × 7½ × 2 inches. Sprinkle with salt. Place dill weed sprig and lemon slice on each. Top with peppercorns. Pour wine over fish. Bake uncovered 20 to 25 minutes or until fish flakes easily.

4 servings

PER STEAK: Calories 200; Protein 35 g; Carbohydrate 1 g; Fat 4 g; Cholesterol 55 g; Sodium 230 mg

MICROWAVE DIRECTIONS: Prepare as directed—except arrange fish steaks, thickest parts to outside edges, in rectangular microwavable dish, 12 × 7½ × 2 inches. Cover tightly and microwave on high 7 to 9 minutes, rotating dish ½ turn after 4 minutes, until fish flakes easily with fork. Let stand covered 3 minutes; drain.

Tuna with Vegetables

1 small eggplant (about 1 pound), cut
   into ½-inch pieces
2 medium stalks celery, sliced (about
   1 cup)
1 large onion, sliced
1 medium green bell pepper, chopped
   (about 1 cup)
3 tablespoons olive or vegetable oil
3 tablespoons red wine vinegar
2 teaspoons sugar
1 teaspoon dried basil leaves
½ teaspoon dried oregano leaves
¼ teaspoon salt
3 medium tomatoes, chopped (about
   2½ cups)
2 cans (6½ ounces each) tuna in water,
   drained
¼ cup snipped fresh parsley
¼ cup grated Parmesan cheese

Cook eggplant, celery, onion and bell pepper in oil in 10-inch skillet over medium heat, stirring occasionally, until onion is tender, about 5 minutes. Stir in vinegar, sugar, basil, oregano and salt. Heat to boiling; reduce heat.

Cover and simmer until eggplant is tender, about 7 minutes. Stir in tomatoes and tuna. Heat uncovered, stirring occasionally, just until tuna is hot, about 5 minutes. Stir in parsley; sprinkle with cheese.

6 servings

PER SERVING: Calories 215; Protein 19 g; Carbohydrate 14 g; Fat 9 g; Cholesterol 15 mg; Sodium 380 mg

Mahimahi in Fennel Sauce

1½ pounds mahimahi or other lean fish
    fillets
2 tablespoons olive oil
2 tablespoons margarine or butter
½ cup chopped fennel bulb
¼ cup chopped onion (about 1 small)
¼ teaspoon salt
⅛ teaspoon pepper

Heat oven to 450°. If fish fillets are large, cut into 6 serving pieces. Arrange fish in ungreased rectangular baking dish, 12 × 7½ × 2 inches. Heat oil and margarine in 1-quart saucepan over medium-high heat. Sauté remaining ingredients in oil about 2 minutes. Spoon over fish. Bake 12 to 17 minutes or until fish flakes easily with fork. **6 servings**

PER SERVING: Calories 130; Protein 20 g; Carbohydrate 0 g; Fat 5 g; Cholesterol 35 mg; Sodium 90 mg

MICROWAVE DIRECTIONS: Arrange fish fillets, thickest parts to outside edges, in rectangular microwavable dish, 12 × 7½ × 2 inches. Place remaining ingredients in 4-cup microwavable measure. Cover fennel mixture tightly and microwave on high 2 minutes, stirring after 1 minute. Spoon over fish. Cover fish tightly and microwave 8 to 10 minutes, rotating dish ½ turn after 4 minutes, until fish flakes easily with fork. Let stand covered 3 minutes.

Gingered Tuna Steaks

These steaks are also great on the grill!

¼ cup margarine or butter, melted
1 tablespoon dry sherry or chicken broth
1 tablespoon soy sauce
1 tablespoon grated gingerroot
6 small albacore tuna or other fatty fish
    steaks, about 1 inch thick (about
    2 pounds)

Mix margarine, sherry, soy sauce and gingerroot. Set oven control to broil. Brush fish steaks with half of the margarine mixture. Broil fish with tops about 4 inches from heat 9 minutes. Turn fish carefully and brush with remaining margarine mixture. Broil about 9 minutes or until fish flakes easily with fork. **6 servings**

PER STEAK: Calories 265; Protein 33 g; Carbohydrate 0 g; Fat 13 g; Cholesterol 55 mg; Sodium 360 mg

MICROWAVE DIRECTIONS: Place fish steaks in rectangular microwavable dish, 12 × 7½ × 2 inches. Pour margarine mixture over fish. Cover tightly and microwave on high 9 to 11 minutes, rotating dish ½ turn after 4 minutes, until fish flakes easily with fork. Let stand covered 3 minutes.

Sesame Perch

1 pound ocean perch or other lean fish fillets
¼ teaspoon salt
2 tablespoons margarine or butter
2 tablespoons vegetable oil
1 tablespoon sesame seed
1 lemon, cut in half
1 tablespoon chopped fresh or 1 teaspoon dried basil leaves
2 tablespoons snipped fresh parsley

If fish fillets are large, cut into 4 serving pieces. Sprinkle both sides with salt. Heat margarine and oil in 10-inch skillet over medium heat until hot. Cook fish about 10 minutes, carefully turning once, until brown on both sides. Remove fish and keep warm.

Cook and stir sesame seed in same skillet over medium heat about 5 minutes or until golden brown; remove from heat. Squeeze lemon over sesame seed. Stir in basil. Pour over fish. Sprinkle with parsley. **4 servings**

PER SERVING: Calories 215; Protein 20 g; Carbohydrate 1 g; Fat 15 g; Cholesterol 30 mg; Sodium 205 mg

---

Swordfish with Cucumber

1½-pound swordfish steak, about 1 inch thick
¼ cup lemon juice
2 tablespoons olive or vegetable oil
2 cloves garlic, crushed
¼ teaspoon chili powder
⅛ teaspoon ground cloves
½ teaspoon salt
1 large cucumber
1 tablespoon olive or vegetable oil
1 tablespoon lemon juice
⅛ teaspoon salt
¼ teaspoon fennel seed

Cut fish steak into 6 serving pieces. Place in ungreased square baking dish, 8 × 8 × 2 inches. Mix ¼ cup lemon juice, 2 tablespoons oil, the garlic, chili powder, cloves and ½ teaspoon salt; pour over fish. Cover and refrigerate at least 2 hours.

Cut cucumber lengthwise into fourths; remove seeds. Cut each fourth lengthwise into thin slices. Remove fish from marinade; reserve marinade. Place fish on rack in broiler pan. Set oven control to broil. Broil fish with tops 2 to 3 inches from heat until light brown, about 5 minutes. Turn carefully; brush with marinade. Broil until fish flakes easily with fork, 5 to 8 minutes longer.

Heat 1 tablespoon oil in 10-inch skillet over medium heat until hot. Add cucumber. Cook and stir just until cucumber is crisp-tender, about 2 minutes. Toss with 1 tablespoon lemon juice, ⅛ teaspoon salt and the fennel seed. Serve with fish. **6 servings**

PER SERVING: Calories 145; Protein 19 g; Carbohydrate 2 g; Fat 7 g; Cholesterol 55 mg; Sodium 120 mg

---

Red Snapper Stew

Red Snapper Stew

1 medium onion, sliced
1 tablespoon reduced-calorie margarine
4 cups chicken broth
1 cup ¼-inch slices carrots (about
   2 medium)
½ cup uncooked regular rice
1 tablespoon lemon juice
½ teaspoon salt
¼ teaspoon dried dill weed
1 teaspoon chopped fresh or ¼ teaspoon
   dried thyme leaves
¼ teaspoon pepper
1 package (10 ounces) frozen baby Brussels sprouts
1½ pounds red snapper or other lean
   fish fillets, cut into 1-inch pieces
1 cup sliced mushrooms (about
   3 ounces)

Cook and stir onion in margarine in Dutch oven over medium heat until onion is tender, about 5 minutes. Stir in broth, carrots, rice, lemon juice, salt, dill weed, thyme and pepper. Heat to boiling; reduce heat. Cover and simmer until rice is tender, about 20 minutes.

Rinse Brussels sprouts under running cold water to separate; drain. Stir into rice mixture. Heat to boiling; reduce heat. Simmer uncovered 5 minutes. Stir in fish and mushrooms; simmer until fish flakes easily with fork, 5 to 8 minutes longer. **4 servings**

PER SERVING: Calories 320; Protein 33 g; Carbohydrate 33 g; Fat 6 g; Cholesterol 40 mg; Sodium 1160 mg

Shaping Up Your Recipes

Look for ways to curb calories in your favorite recipes by following this checklist.

• Are there any lower-fat or lower-calorie ingredients that can be substituted in the recipe?
• Skim milk for regular milk?
• Reduced-calorie mayonnaise for regular mayonnaise?
• Neufchâtel cheese for cream cheese?
• Nondairy whipped topping for whipped cream?
• Plain low-fat or nonfat yogurt for sour cream?
• Can the recipe be cooked another way— grilled, broiled, steamed, microwaved, oven-fried, or panfried with a small amount of fat or with nonstick cooking spray?

Cold Poached Salmon

A wonderful meal for hot weather.

2 cups water
1 cup dry white wine or chicken broth
1 small onion, sliced
1 medium stalk celery (with leaves), chopped
1/2 teaspoon salt
1/4 teaspoon dried thyme leaves
1/4 teaspoon dried tarragon leaves
5 peppercorns
4 sprigs parsley
1 bay leaf
4 salmon steaks, 1 inch thick (about 2 pounds)
Green Sauce (right)

Heat water, wine, onion, celery, salt, thyme, tarragon, peppercorns, parsley and bay leaf to boiling in 12-inch skillet; reduce heat. Cover and simmer 5 minutes. Place fish in skillet; add water, if necessary, to cover. Heat to boiling; reduce heat.

Simmer until fish flakes easily with fork, 12 to 15 minutes. Carefully remove fish with slotted spatula; place on wire rack to drain. Carefully remove skin; cut fish lengthwise into halves. Cover and refrigerate until cold, at least 4 hours. Prepare Green Sauce; serve with fish.

8 servings

PER SERVING: Calories 185; Protein 27 g; Carbohydrate 3 g; Fat 7 g; Cholesterol 40 mg; Sodium 390 mg

Green Sauce

1 cup parsley sprigs
1 1/2 cups large curd creamed cottage cheese
1 tablespoon lemon juice
1 tablespoon milk
1/2 teaspoon dried basil leaves
1/2 teaspoon salt
1/8 teaspoon pepper
4 to 6 drops red pepper sauce

Place all ingredients in blender container. Cover and blend on high speed, stopping blender occasionally to scrape sides, until smooth, about 3 minutes.

MICROWAVE DIRECTIONS: Rinse fish steaks under gently running cold water. Place fish in ungreased rectangular microwavable dish, 12 × 7 1/2 × 2 inches. Place onion, celery, salt, thyme, tarragon, peppercorns, parsley and bay leaf on fish. Pour 1 cup water and 1/2 cup wine over fish. Cover tightly and microwave on high 3 minutes; rotate dish 1/2 turn. Microwave until small ends of fish flake easily with fork, 5 to 7 minutes. Let stand covered 3 minutes. Continue as directed.

Shrimp with Feta Cheese

Feta cheese is Greek in origin and is readily available in most supermarkets.

1 pound fresh or frozen raw medium-size shrimp (in shells)
1 cup chopped onion (about 1 large)
2 cloves garlic, chopped
3 tablespoons olive or vegetable oil
½ cup dry white wine or chicken broth
1 tablespoon chopped fresh or 1 teaspoon dried basil leaves
1 tablespoon chopped fresh or 1 teaspoon dried oregano leaves
Dash of ground red pepper (cayenne)
1 can (28 ounces) Italian pear-shaped tomatoes, drained and chopped
2 tablespoons lemon juice
2 ounces feta cheese, crumbled
Chopped fresh parsley

Peel shrimp. (If shrimp are frozen, do not thaw; peel in cold water.) Make a shallow cut lengthwise down back of each shrimp; wash out vein. Cook onion and garlic in oil in 10-inch skillet over medium heat, stirring occasionally, until onion is softened.

Stir in wine, basil, oregano, red pepper and tomatoes. Heat to boiling; reduce heat. Simmer uncovered 20 minutes. Stir in shrimp and lemon juice. Cover and cook 3 to 5 minutes or until shrimp are pink. Sprinkle with cheese and parsley. Serve with hot cooked rice if desired.

4 servings

PER SERVING: Calories 340; Protein 23 g; Carbohydrate 28 g; Fat 14 g; Cholesterol 295 mg; Sodium 1040 mg

Stir-fried Garlic Shrimp

2 large cloves garlic, finely chopped
2 teaspoons vegetable oil
1 pound frozen, peeled and deveined medium-size raw shrimp, thawed
3 cups sliced mushrooms (about 8 ounces)
1 cup 1-inch pieces green onions (with tops)
¼ cup dry white wine or chicken broth
2 cups hot cooked rice

Cook and stir garlic in oil in 10-inch nonstick skillet over medium-high heat 1 minute. Add shrimp; stir-fry 1 minute. Stir in mushrooms, onions and wine; stir-fry until shrimp are pink and vegetables are hot, about 2 minutes longer. Serve over rice.

4 servings

PER SERVING: Calories 230; Protein 16 g; Carbohydrate 30 g; Fat 5 g; Cholesterol 210 mg; Sodium 490 mg

Scallops with Red Pepper Sauce

You can use yellow peppers instead of red if you like.

1 large red bell pepper, cut into fourths
⅛ teaspoon salt
10 drops red pepper sauce
1 clove garlic, finely chopped
¼ cup plain nonfat yogurt
1 pound bay scallops
¼ cup sliced green onions (with tops)
Fresh cilantro leaves

Place steamer basket in ½ inch water in saucepan or skillet (water should not touch bottom of basket). Place bell pepper in basket. Cover tightly and heat to boiling; reduce heat. Steam 8 to 10 minutes or until tender.

Place bell pepper, salt, pepper sauce and garlic in blender or food processor. Cover and blend or process on medium speed until almost smooth. Heat in 1-quart saucepan over medium heat, stirring occasionally, until hot; remove from heat. Gradually stir in yogurt; keep warm.

Spray 10-inch nonstick skillet with nonstick cooking spray. Heat over medium-high heat. Add scallops and onions; stir-fry 4 to 5 minutes or until scallops are white in center. Serve sauce with scallops. Garnish with cilantro.

4 servings

PER SERVING: Calories 115; Protein 20 g; Carbohydrate 6 g; Fat 1 g; Cholesterol 35 mg; Sodium 270 mg

MICROWAVE DIRECTIONS: Prepare bell pepper as directed—except place in 1-quart microwavable casserole. Add ¼ cup water. Cover tightly and microwave on high 4 to 5 minutes, stirring after 2 minutes, until tender; drain. Blend as directed. Pour into 1-quart microwavable casserole. Cover tightly and microwave on high 30 to 60 seconds or until hot. Stir in yogurt. Mix scallops and onions in 1½-quart microwavable casserole. Cover tightly and microwave on high 4 to 6 minutes, stirring every 2 minutes, until scallops are white in center; drain.

Scallops with Red Pepper Sauce

Mussels with Mustard Sauce

Mussels are quite easy to clean. Discard any with open or broken shells. Scrub the remaining mussels with a stiff brush under cold running water, then remove the fibrous thread (the "beard").

2 cloves garlic, chopped
1/2 teaspoon cracked black pepper
1 teaspoon olive or vegetable oil
1/2 cup dry red wine or beef broth
2 pounds mussels (about 8 dozen)
1/4 cup snipped parsley
Mustard Sauce (below)

Cook and stir garlic and pepper in oil in 4-quart nonstick Dutch oven until garlic is softened. Add wine; heat to boiling. Add mussels and parsley. Cover and heat to boiling; reduce heat. Simmer until mussels open, 5 to 10 minutes. Stir to coat with liquid. Prepare Mustard Sauce; serve with mussels.

4 servings

PER SERVING: Calories 125; Protein 14 g; Carbohydrate 7 g; Fat 4 g; Cholesterol 14 mg; Sodium 125 mg

Mustard Sauce

1/2 cup nonfat plain yogurt
2 tablespoons Dijon mustard
1 tablespoon reduced-calorie sour cream
1 teaspoon honey

Heat all ingredients, stirring occasionally, just until hot (do not boil).

Noodles with White Clam Sauce

1 medium onion, chopped (about 1/2 cup)
1 clove garlic, crushed
3 tablespoons margarine
3 tablespoons all-purpose flour
3 cans (6 1/2 ounces each) minced clams, undrained
1/2 teaspoon salt
1/2 teaspoon dried basil
1/8 teaspoon pepper
1/4 cup snipped parsley
4 to 5 cups hot cooked noodles
Grated Parmesan cheese

Cook and stir onion and garlic in margarine in 2-quart saucepan until onion is tender. Stir in flour. Stir in clams, salt, basil and pepper. Heat to boiling; reduce heat. Cover and simmer 5 minutes. Stir in parsley. Serve over noodles. Sprinkle with cheese.

6 servings

PER SERVING: Calories 255; Protein 13 g; Carbohydrate 33 g; Fat 8 g; Cholesterol 35 mg; Sodium 490 mg

MICROWAVE DIRECTIONS: Place onion, garlic and margarine in 2-quart microwavable casserole. Microwave uncovered on high 2 to 3 minutes or until onion is transparent. Stir in flour. Stir in clams, salt, basil and pepper. Microwave uncovered 5 to 6 minutes, stirring every 2 minutes, until slightly thickened and bubbly. Stir in parsley. Let stand on flat, heatproof surface 5 minutes (not on wire rack).

Seafood Lasagne

½ cup margarine or butter
2 cloves garlic, crushed
½ cup all-purpose flour
½ teaspoon salt
2 cups milk
2 cups chicken broth
2 cups shredded mozzarella cheese
  (8 ounces)
½ cup sliced green onions (with tops)
1 tablespoon chopped fresh or 1 teaspoon dried basil leaves
¼ teaspoon pepper
8 ounces uncooked lasagne noodles
  (9 or 10 noodles)
1 cup small curd creamed cottage
  cheese
1 cup cooked crabmeat or ½-inch pieces
  imitation crabmeat
1 cup bite-size pieces cooked shrimp
½ cup grated Parmesan cheese

Heat oven to 350°. Heat margarine in 3-quart saucepan over low heat until melted. Add garlic. Stir in flour and salt. Cook, stirring constantly, until bubbly; remove from heat. Stir in milk and broth. Heat to boiling, stirring constantly. Boil and stir 1 minute. Stir in mozzarella cheese, onions, basil and pepper. Cook over low heat, stirring constantly, until cheese is melted.

Spread ¼ of the cheese sauce (about 1½ cups) in ungreased rectangular baking dish, 13 × 9 × 2 inches. Top with 3 or 4 uncooked noodles, overlapping if necessary. Spread cottage cheese over noodles in dish. Repeat with ¼ of the cheese sauce and 3 or 4 noodles. Top with crabmeat, shrimp and ¼ of the cheese sauce. Top with remaining noodles and cheese sauce. Sprinkle with Parmesan cheese.

Bake uncovered 35 to 40 minutes or until noodles are tender. Let stand 15 minutes before cutting. **12 servings**

PER SERVING: Calories 285; Protein 16 g; Carbohydrate 19 g; Fat 16 g; Cholesterol 60 mg; Sodium 650 mg.

Cajun Seafood and Noodles

Cajun Seafood and Noodles

If frozen shrimp and crab are not readily available, use canned shrimp and crab, which are just as delicious.

6 ounces uncooked noodles (about
   3 cups)
1 tablespoon vegetable oil
¾ cup chopped green bell pepper (about
   1 medium)
½ cup chopped onion (about 1 medium)
2 tablespoons chopped fresh parsley
⅛ teaspoon ground red pepper (cayenne)
⅛ teaspoon pepper
2 cloves garlic, finely chopped
1 tablespoon all-purpose flour
1 can (16 ounces) whole tomatoes,
   undrained
1 package (10 ounces) frozen cut okra,
   thawed
1 package (6 ounces) frozen cooked
   small shrimp, thawed and drained
1 package (6 ounces) frozen crabmeat,
   thawed, drained and cartilage removed

Cook noodles as directed on package; drain. Heat oil in 10-inch nonstick skillet over medium heat. Cook bell pepper, onion, parsley, red pepper, pepper and garlic 3 minutes, stirring frequently. Stir in flour and tomatoes; break up tomatoes.

Cook uncovered, stirring frequently, until mixture thickens and boils. Stir in okra, shrimp and crabmeat. Cook uncovered 5 minutes, stirring occasionally. Serve over noodles.

6 servings

PER SERVING: Calories 225; Protein 15 g; Carbohydrate 31 g; Fat 5 g; Cholesterol 85 mg; Sodium 240 mg

Seafood-stuffed Shells

15 uncooked jumbo macaroni shells
2 cups small curd creamed cottage
   cheese
¼ cup plus 2 tablespoons milk
1 tablespoon lemon juice
½ teaspoon salt
⅛ teaspoon pepper
½ cup snipped parsley
½ teaspoon dried basil leaves
2 cloves garlic, crushed
2 medium stalks celery, sliced (about
   1 cup)
1 medium zucchini, coarsely shredded
1 medium onion, chopped (about ½ cup)
6 imitation crabmeat sticks, cut into
   ½-inch pieces
2 cans (4¼ ounces each) large shrimp,
   rinsed and drained
Salad greens

Prepare macaroni shells as directed on package; refrigerate until chilled, at least 1 hour.

Place cottage cheese, milk, lemon juice, salt and pepper in blender container. Cover and blend on high speed, stopping blender occasionally to scrape sides, until smooth, about 2 minutes. Remove ½ cup; reserve. Add parsley, basil and garlic to remaining mixture in blender container. Cover and blend on high speed until smooth, about 45 seconds; refrigerate.

Mix celery, zucchini, onion, seafood pieces, shrimp and reserved ½ cup cottage cheese mixture. Spoon into macaroni shells. Refrigerate at least 1 hour.

Place stuffed shells on salad greens; serve parsley mixture with shells. (If parsley mixture is too thick, stir in additional milk until of desired consistency.) **5 servings**

PER SERVING: Calories 425; Protein 36 g; Carbohydrate 55 g; Fat 7 g; Cholesterol 110 mg; Sodium 2210 mg

Curried Chicken and Nectarines

3

Pleasing Poultry and Meatless Main Dishes

Curried Chicken and Nectarines

4 boneless skinless chicken breast
   halves (about 1 pound)
2 tablespoons reduced-calorie oil-and-
   vinegar dressing
1 teaspoon curry powder
¼ cup raisins
¼ cup sliced green onions (with tops)
¼ teaspoon salt
1 medium bell pepper, cut into ¼-inch
   strips
2 small nectarines, cut into ¼-inch slices

Trim fat from chicken breast halves. Cut chicken crosswise into ½-inch strips. Mix dressing and curry powder in medium bowl. Add chicken; toss. Heat 10-inch nonstick skillet over medium-high heat. Stir in chicken and remaining ingredients except nectarines; stir-fry 4 to 6 minutes or until chicken is done. Stir in nectarines carefully; heat through. Serve with hot cooked rice or couscous if desired.   **4 servings**

PER SERVING: Calories 210; Protein 25 g; Carbohydrate 15 g; Fat 6 g; Cholesterol 80 mg; Sodium 230 mg

MICROWAVE DIRECTIONS: Prepare chicken as directed. Mix dressing and curry powder in 2-quart microwavable casserole. Add chicken; toss. Stir in remaining ingredients except nectarines. Cover tightly and microwave on high 8 to 10 minutes, stirring after 4 minutes, until chicken is done. Stir in nectarines carefully. Cover and microwave 1 minute or until heated through.

Hot Chicken Salad with Plum Sauce

2 teaspoons olive or vegetable oil
4 skinless boneless chicken breast
    halves (about 1 pound)
1 can (16 ounces) purple plums in juice,
    rinsed, drained and pitted
1 tablespoon lemon juice
2 teaspoons packed brown sugar
1/4 teaspoon ground ginger
1/8 teaspoon crushed red pepper
1 clove garlic
4 cups shredded Chinese cabbage
1 cup bean sprouts (about 2 ounces)
1 tablespoon thinly sliced green onion
    with top (about 1/2 medium)

Heat oil in 10-inch nonstick skillet over medium heat. Cook chicken breast halves, turning once, about 10 minutes or until done.

Place remaining ingredients except cabbage, bean sprouts and onion in blender or food processor. Cover and blend on high speed or process about 30 seconds or until smooth. Heat sauce if desired.

Arrange cabbage, bean sprouts and onion on 4 serving plates. Top with chicken. Spoon plum sauce over chicken.   **4 servings**

PER SERVING: Calories 220; Protein 28 g; Carbohydrate 16 g; Fat 4 g; Cholesterol 65 mg; Sodium 140 mg

Lemon Chicken

6 small boneless skinless chicken breast
    halves (about 1 1/2 pounds)
1/4 cup margarine
1/2 cup dry white wine or chicken broth
1 tablespoon lemon juice
1/4 teaspoon salt
1/8 teaspoon dried dill weed
1/2 lemon, thinly sliced
2 green onions (with tops), sliced

Cook chicken breast halves in margarine in 10-inch skillet about 5 minutes on each side, turning once, until light brown. Mix wine, lemon juice, salt and dill weed; pour over chicken. Place lemon slices on chicken.

Heat to boiling; reduce heat. Cover and simmer 10 to 15 minutes or until chicken is done. Remove chicken; keep warm. Heat wine mixture to boiling; cook about 3 minutes or until reduced to about half. Pour over chicken. Sprinkle with onions.   **6 servings**

PER SERVING: Calories 250; Protein 24 g; Carbohydrate 2 g; Fat 11 g; Cholesterol 80 mg; Sodium 270 mg

MICROWAVE DIRECTIONS: Prepare chicken as directed—except decrease margarine to 2 tablespoons and wine to 1/4 cup. Place margarine in 3-quart microwavable casserole. Microwave uncovered on high about 1 minute 30 seconds or until melted. Arrange chicken, thickest parts to outside edge, in margarine. Cover tightly and microwave 4 minutes.

Mix wine, lemon juice, salt and dill weed; pour over chicken. Place lemon slices on chicken; rotate casserole 1/2 turn. Cover tightly and microwave 4 to 6 minutes or until chicken is done. Let stand covered 5 minutes. Sprinkle with onions.

Chicken Breasts Dijon

Different types of mustard will make subtle and delicious changes in the flavor of this dish. You may want to try a robust, grainy German mustard, or use a light champagne mustard for more delicate flavor.

6 small chicken breast halves (about 3 pounds), skinned and boned
¼ cup Dijon mustard
1 teaspoon vegetable oil
2 tablespoons dry white wine or chicken broth
Freshly ground pepper
2 tablespoons mustard seed

Heat oven to 400°. Remove excess fat from chicken. Place chicken, meaty sides up, in rectangular pan, 13 × 9 × 2 inches, sprayed with nonstick cooking spray. Mix mustard, oil and wine; brush over chicken. Sprinkle with pepper and mustard seed. Bake uncovered until chicken is done, about 30 minutes. Sprinkle with snipped parsley if desired. **6 servings**

PER SERVING: Calories 270; Protein 46 g; Carbohydrate 2 g; Fat 7 g; Cholesterol 120 mg; Sodium 230 mg
---

Peanutty Chicken Kabobs

The unusual sauce for these kabobs comes from an old standby—the crunchy peanut butter in your cupboard.

1 pound boneless skinless chicken breast halves or thighs
⅓ cup crunchy peanut butter
⅓ cup boiling water
1 tablespoon grated gingerroot or 1 teaspoon ground ginger
1 tablespoon lemon juice
⅛ teaspoon crushed red pepper

Cut chicken into 1½-inch pieces. Mix remaining ingredients. Reserve ¼ cup. Set oven control to broil. Thread chicken cubes on four 11-inch metal skewers, leaving space between each. Brush chicken with half of the reserved peanut butter mixture.

Broil chicken with tops about 4 inches from heat about 5 minutes or until brown. Turn and brush with remaining reserved peanut butter mixture. Broil 5 minutes or until golden brown. Serve with peanut butter mixture and chopped peanuts if desired. **4 servings**

PER KABOB: Calories 215; Protein 21 g; Carbohydrate 5 g; Fat 12 g; Cholesterol 45 mg; Sodium 140 mg
---

TO GRILL: Cover and grill kabobs 4 to 5 inches from medium coals 15 to 25 minutes, turning and brushing with peanut butter mixture, until golden brown.

Orange Stir-fried Chicken

Orange Stir-fried Chicken

4 boneless skinless chicken breast
   halves (about 1 pound)
1 tablespoon low-sodium soy sauce
1 teaspoon cornstarch
1 teaspoon grated gingerroot or ½ teaspoon ground ginger
1 clove garlic, finely chopped
½ cup orange juice
2 teaspoons cornstarch
2 teaspoons vegetable oil
3 cups thinly sliced fresh mushrooms
   (about 8 ounces)
½ cup coarsely shredded carrot (about
   1 medium)
2 cups hot cooked rice

Trim fat from chicken breast halves. Cut chicken
into ¼-inch strips. Mix soy sauce, 1 teaspoon
cornstarch, the gingerroot and garlic in medium
glass or plastic bowl. Stir in chicken. Cover and
refrigerate 30 minutes.

Mix orange juice and 2 teaspoons cornstarch
until cornstarch is dissolved. Heat 1 teaspoon of
the oil in 10-inch nonstick skillet over high heat.
Add chicken mixture; stir-fry until chicken turns
white. Remove chicken from skillet.

Add remaining 1 teaspoon oil to skillet. Add
mushrooms and carrot; stir-fry about 3 minutes
or until mushrooms are tender. Stir in chicken
and orange juice mixture. Heat to boiling, stirring
constantly. Boil and stir 30 seconds or until thickened. Serve over rice.

4 servings

PER SERVING: Calories 315; Protein 28 g; Carbohydrate 35 g; Fat 6 g; Cholesterol 80 mg; Sodium 630 mg

Broiled Chicken

3- to 3½-pound broiler-fryer chicken, cut
   into quarters or pieces
2 tablespoons margarine or butter,
   melted

Fold wing tips across back side of chicken quarters. Set oven control to broil. Brush chicken with
1 tablespoon margarine. Place chicken, skin
sides down, on rack in broiler pan. Place broiler
pan so top of chicken is 7 to 9 inches from heat.
Broil 30 minutes. Sprinkle with salt and pepper.
Turn chicken and brush with 1 tablespoon margarine. Broil 15 to 25 minutes longer or until
chicken is brown and juices run clear.

6 servings

PER SERVING: Calories 260; Protein 28 g; Carbohydrate 0 g; Fat 16 g; Cholesterol 90 mg; Sodium 105 mg

TO GRILL: Cover and grill chicken, bone sides
down, 5 to 6 inches from medium coals 40 to
60 minutes, turning and brushing with margarine, until juices run clear.

BROILED LEMON CHICKEN: Do not brush with margarine or butter. Cut 1 lemon in half. Rub and
squeeze lemon over chicken. Brush with 2 tablespoons margarine or butter, melted. Mix ½ teaspoon salt, ½ teaspoon paprika and ⅛ teaspoon
pepper. Sprinkle over chicken. Broil as directed.

Herbed Chicken

2 tablespoons margarine or butter
2 tablespoons olive or vegetable oil
¼ cup finely chopped onion (about
    1 small)
¼ cup lemon juice
2 tablespoons Worcestershire sauce
1½ teaspoons chopped fresh or ½ tea-
    spoon dried basil leaves
¾ teaspoon chopped fresh or ¼ tea-
    spoon dried marjoram leaves
¾ teaspoon chopped fresh or ¼ tea-
    spoon dried oregano leaves
2 large cloves garlic, finely chopped
3- to 3½-pound broiler-fryer chicken, cut
    up

Heat oven to 375°. Heat margarine and oil in rectangular pan, 13 × 9 × 2 inches, in oven until margarine is melted. Stir in remaining ingredients except chicken. Place chicken in pan, turning to coat with herb mixture. Arrange chicken pieces skin sides up. Bake uncovered 30 minutes. Turn chicken. Bake about 30 minutes longer or until juices run clear.

6 servings

PER SERVING: Calories 345; Protein 28 g; Carbohydrate 3 g; Fat 22 g; Cholesterol 90 mg; Sodium 180 mg

MICROWAVE DIRECTIONS: Place margarine and oil in rectangular microwavable dish, 12 × 7½ × 2 inches. Microwave uncovered on high 45 to 60 seconds or until margarine is melted. Stir in remaining ingredients except chicken. Place chicken in dish, turning to coat with herb mixture. Arrange chicken, skin sides up and thickest parts to outside edges, in dish. Cover with waxed paper and microwave on high 16 to 20 minutes, rotating dish ½ turn after 10 minutes, until juices run clear.

Oven-barbecued Chicken

Great when you can't get the grill out to barbecue!

3- to 3½-pound broiler-fryer chicken, cut
    up
¾ cup chili sauce
2 tablespoons honey
2 tablespoons soy sauce
1 teaspoon dry mustard
½ teaspoon prepared horseradish
½ teaspoon red pepper sauce

Heat oven to 375°. Place chicken, skin sides up, in ungreased rectangular pan, 13 × 9 × 2 inches. Mix remaining ingredients. Pour over chicken. Cover and bake 30 minutes. Spoon sauce over chicken. Bake uncovered about 30 minutes longer or until juices of chicken run clear.

6 servings

PER SERVING: Calories 305; Protein 29 g; Carbohydrate 14 g; Fat 14 g; Cholesterol 90 mg; Sodium 830 mg

Chicken with Vegetables

2½- to 3-pound broiler-fryer chicken, cut up
1 teaspoon salt
1 teaspoon paprika
2 tablespoons vegetable oil
3 medium tomatoes, cut into wedges
2 cloves garlic, finely chopped
1 medium zucchini, cut into ¼-inch slices
1 medium onion, chopped (about ½ cup)
1 can (17 ounces) whole kernel corn, drained
1 tablespoon dried oregano leaves
1 teaspoon chili powder
½ teaspoon ground cumin

Remove skin from chicken. Sprinkle chicken with salt and paprika. Heat oil in 12-inch skillet or Dutch oven. Cook chicken in oil over medium heat 15 to 20 minutes or until light brown on all sides; reduce heat. Cover and cook 20 minutes. Stir in remaining ingredients. Heat to boiling; reduce heat. Cover and simmer 5 to 10 minutes or until zucchini is crisp-tender. Remove vegetables with slotted spoon. Serve with chicken.   **7 servings**

PER SERVING: Calories 240; Protein 24 g; Carbohydrate 14 g; Fat 10 g; Cholesterol 70 mg; Sodium 390 mg

Arroz con Pollo

In Spanish, this means "chicken with rice." It's an easy one-dish meal that's satisfying and hearty.

2½- to 3-pound broiler-fryer chicken, cut up
¾ teaspoon salt
¼ to ½ teaspoon paprika
¼ teaspoon pepper
2½ cups chicken broth
1 cup uncooked regular long grain rice
1 medium onion, chopped (about ½ cup)
2 cloves garlic, crushed
1½ teaspoons chopped fresh or ½ teaspoon dried oregano leaves
⅛ teaspoon ground turmeric
1 bay leaf
1 package (10 ounces) frozen green peas, thawed and drained

Heat oven to 350°. Place chicken, skin sides up, in ungreased rectangular baking dish, 13 × 9 × 2 inches. Sprinkle with salt, paprika and pepper. Bake uncovered 30 minutes.

Heat broth to boiling. Remove chicken from baking dish; drain fat from baking dish. Mix broth, rice, onion, garlic, oregano, turmeric, bay leaf and peas in baking dish. Top with chicken. Cover with aluminum foil and bake about 30 minutes or until rice and thickest pieces of chicken are done and liquid is absorbed. Remove bay leaf. Garnish with pimiento strips and olives if desired.   **6 servings**

PER SERVING: Calories 230; Protein 30 g; Carbohydrate 9 g; Fat 7 g; Cholesterol 80 mg; Sodium 730 mg

Herbed Cornish Hens

Herbed Cornish Hens

These compact birds, full of white meat, are great to serve when you have company for dinner.

3 Rock Cornish hens (about 1 pound each)
1 cup herb-seasoned croutons
¼ cup sliced ripe olives
2 tablespoons lemon juice
2 tablespoons vinegar
1 tablespoon vegetable oil
1 teaspoon fresh or ¼ teaspoon dried thyme leaves
¼ teaspoon salt
1 clove garlic, crushed

Heat oven to 350°. Dry cavities of hens (do not rub cavities with salt). Mix croutons and olives. Stuff each hen loosely with ⅓ cup stuffing; fasten openings with skewers and lace shut with string. Place hens, breast sides up, in shallow baking pan.

Mix remaining ingredients; pour over hens. Roast uncovered until hens are done, spooning lemon mixture over hens every 20 minutes, about 2 hours. To serve, cut hens into halves along backbone from tail to neck.

6 servings

PER SERVING: Calories 210; Protein 29 g; Carbohydrate 6 g; Fat 8 g; Cholesterol 100 mg; Sodium 300 mg

Trim Chicken

Just because you are watching your calories doesn't mean you can't have fried chicken every so often—but you should remove the skin before eating. If you do make the switch from a fried chicken breast to a skinless broiled chicken breast, you save 80 calories for a 3-ounce portion. You save 40 calories by broiling instead of frying and another 40 calories by removing the skin. You'll also find that the same size serving of light meat has less fat than dark chicken meat. Chicken is a favorite dish, especially for calorie watchers, and you'll find some of the best recipes for chicken right here.

Madeira-sauced Chicken Wings

12 chicken wings (about 2 pounds)
¾ cup water
⅓ cup Madeira*
⅓ cup chopped onion
2 teaspoons finely shredded orange peel
¼ teaspoon salt
2 cloves garlic, finely chopped
2 teaspoons cornstarch
3 slices bacon, crisply cooked and crumbled

Cut each chicken wing at joints to make 3 pieces; discard tips. Cut off excess skin; discard. Place chicken, water, Madeira, onion, orange peel, salt and garlic in glass bowl or plastic bag. Cover bowl or seal bag tightly. Refrigerate at least 2 hours.

Drain chicken, reserving marinade. Set oven control to broil. Place chicken on rack in broiler pan. Place broiler pan so top of chicken is 5 to 7 inches from heat. Broil about 10 minutes, turning once, until juices run clear.

Mix ¼ cup reserved marinade and the cornstarch in 1½-quart saucepan. Stir in remaining marinade. Cook over low heat, stirring constantly, until mixture thickens. Stir in bacon. Serve with chicken wings.   **4 servings**

⅔ cup orange juice can be substituted for the Madeira. Reduce water to ½ cup.

PER SERVING: Calories 180; Protein 18 g; Carbohydrate 4 g; Fat 6 g; Cholesterol 50 mg; Sodium 225 mg

MICROWAVE DIRECTIONS: Decrease water to ½ cup (¼ cup if substituting orange juice for the Madeira). Place chicken wings in rectangular microwavable dish, 11 × 7 × 1½ inches. Cover with waxed paper and microwave on high 8 to 10 minutes, rotating dish ½ turn after 4 minutes, until juices run clear; drain. Mix ¼ cup reserved marinade and the cornstarch in 4-cup microwavable measure. Stir in remaining marinade. Microwave uncovered on high 3 to 4 minutes or until thickened and boiling. Continue as directed.

Using scissors or sharp knife, cut each chicken wing at joints to make 3 pieces; discard tips.

Garlic Chicken Drummies

2 tablespoons lemon juice
2 tablespoons vegetable oil
1 tablespoon chopped fresh or 1 teaspoon dried oregano leaves
1 clove garlic, finely chopped
8 chicken drumsticks (about 1½ pounds)

Mix all ingredients except chicken drumsticks. Cover and grill chicken 5 to 6 inches from medium coals 15 to 20 minutes; turn chicken. Cover and grill 20 to 40 minutes longer, turning and brushing frequently with garlic mixture, until done.   **4 servings**

PER SERVING: Calories 340; Protein 33 g; Carbohydrate 1 g; Fat 22 g; Cholesterol 140 mg; Sodium 140 mg

Turkey with Chipotle Sauce

Chipotle chilies are ripened, dried and smoked jalapeño chilies. These wrinkled, brown chilies have a smoky flavor and can be purchased in specialty food shops and in the gourmet section of many supermarkets.

Chipotle Sauce (right)
2 teaspoons vegetable oil
1 pound boneless turkey breast slices, cutlets or turkey tenderloin steaks (1/4 to 1/2 inch thick)
3/4 cup chopped seeded tomato (about 1 medium)
2 tablespoons sliced green onion tops

Prepare Chipotle Sauce; keep warm. Heat oil in 10-inch nonstick skillet over medium-high heat until hot. Cook turkey in oil, turning once, until no longer pink, 8 to 10 minutes. Arrange on serving plate; top with Chipotle Sauce. Sprinkle with tomato and green onion tops.

4 servings

PER SERVING: Calories 215; Protein 31 g; Carbohydrate 6 g; Fat 7 g; Cholesterol 75 mg; Sodium 180 mg

Chipotle Sauce

1/2 cup nonfat plain yogurt
2 tablespoons chopped green onions
1 to 2 tablespoons chopped, seeded and drained canned chipotle chilies in adobo sauce
2 tablespoons creamy peanut butter
1/8 teaspoon salt

Place all ingredients in blender container. Cover and blend on medium speed, stopping blender occasionally to scrape sides, until well blended, about 20 seconds. Heat sauce over low heat until hot, stirring occasionally.

NOTE: If turkey pieces are more than 1/2 inch thick, flatten between plastic wrap or waxed paper.

MICROWAVE DIRECTIONS: Prepare Chipotle Sauce as directed; pour into 1-cup microwavable measure. Omit oil; arrange turkey slices on microwavable serving plate. Cover with waxed paper and microwave on medium-high (70%) 4 minutes; rotate plate 1/2 turn. Microwave until no longer pink, 4 to 6 minutes longer. Microwave Chipotle Sauce uncovered on high, stirring every 15 seconds, until hot, about 1 1/2 minutes. Continue as directed.

Glazed Turkey Tenderloins

2 fresh turkey breast tenderloins (about
  1 pound)
1 tablespoon vegetable oil
⅓ cup orange marmalade
1 teaspoon finely chopped gingerroot or
  ½ teaspoon ground ginger
1 teaspoon Worcestershire sauce

Cook turkey in oil in 10-inch skillet over medium heat about 5 minutes or until brown on one side; turn turkey. Stir in marmalade, gingerroot and Worcestershire sauce; reduce heat.

Cover and simmer about 15 minutes, stirring occasionally, until turkey is done and sauce is thickened. Cut turkey into thin slices. Spoon sauce over turkey. **4 servings**

PER SERVING: Calories 230; Protein 25 g; Carbohydrate 19 g; Fat 6 g; Cholesterol 55 mg; Sodium 70 mg

Salad-Bar Strategy

Salad bars, whether at the greengrocer, supermarket, delicatessen or food co-op, are a great convenience. Picking up a ready-made salad for lunch or dinner is always a help to busy calorie counters. Some salad bars provide as many as fifteen or twenty fresh vegetables, washed, trimmed and cut into pieces. Most salad bars also stock such prepared salads as coleslaw, potato salad, Waldorf salad, gelatin-marshmallow molds and other combinations with higher fat contents. Help yourself to only a small amount of those with creamy dressings. Go easy on the cheese cubes, bacon bits, hard-cooked eggs, raisins and croutons, and concentrate on the crisp steamed beans and spinach. This way, you'll have a nutritious treat, not hidden calories!

Cold Poached Turkey with Curry Sauce

Serve this light and fresh turkey dish in hot weather, with such condiments as chutney, raisins and chopped peanuts.

2 turkey tenderloins (about 1½ pounds)
2 tablespoons lemon juice
2 teaspoons chicken bouillon granules
⅛ teaspoon crushed red pepper
1 small onion, cut into fourths
1 clove garlic, cut in half
Curry Sauce (below)
Leaf lettuce

Place turkey tenderloins, lemon juice, bouillon granules (dry), red pepper, onion and garlic in Dutch oven. Add just enough water to cover turkey (2½ to 3 cups). Heat to boiling; reduce heat. Cover and simmer about 30 minutes or until juices run clear. Refrigerate turkey in broth until cool. Prepare Curry Sauce.

Line serving platter with leaf lettuce. Slice turkey diagonally across the grain into ¼-inch slices. Arrange turkey in two rows of overlapping slices on serving platter. Spoon some of the Curry Sauce evenly over turkey. Serve with remaining Curry Sauce. Garnish with tomato wedges and cilantro if desired. **6 servings**

PER SERVING: Calories 175; Protein 27 g; Carbohydrate 6 g; Fat 4 g; Cholesterol 80 mg; Sodium 285 mg

Curry Sauce

1 cup plain yogurt
1 tablespoon chutney
2 teaspoons chopped fresh cilantro
1 teaspoon curry powder
Dash of ground red pepper (cayenne)

Mix all ingredients. Refrigerate.

Turkey Roast with Louisiana Rice

1 teaspoon dry mustard
1 teaspoon ground cumin
½ teaspoon dried thyme leaves
½ teaspoon dried oregano leaves
¼ teaspoon garlic powder
¼ teaspoon pepper
⅛ to ¼ teaspoon ground red pepper (cayenne)
1 tablespoon olive oil
½ cup chopped onion (about 1 medium)
½ cup chopped green bell pepper
½ cup thinly sliced celery
1 cup uncooked converted rice
1 jar (2 ounces) chopped pimientos, drained
2¼ cups chicken broth
2- to 3-pound fresh turkey breast roast (with pop-up thermometer)

Heat oven to 350°. Mix seasonings in small bowl; reserve. Heat oil in 10-inch skillet over medium-high heat until hot. Cook onion, bell pepper and celery in hot oil 1 minute. Stir in rice, pimientos and 1½ teaspoons of the seasoning mixture. Cook and stir 1 minute. Spoon rice mixture into rectangular pan, 13 × 9 × 2 inches. Pour broth over rice mixture.

Place turkey on rice mixture. Pat half of remaining seasoning mixture on turkey underneath skin. Sprinkle remaining seasoning mixture on top of turkey. Cover pan with aluminum foil. Bake about 1¼ hours or until rice is tender and pop-up thermometer pops (165° to 170°). Let stand covered 10 minutes. Slice turkey; serve over rice mixture. **12 servings**

PER SERVING: Calories 175; Protein 22 g; Carbohydrate 11 g; Fat 4 g; Cholesterol 50 mg; Sodium 85 mg

NOTE: If turkey breast roast does not have pop-up thermometer, use meat thermometer inserted in thickest part of turkey. The USDA recommends cooking turkey breast roasts to 170°.

Impossible Turkey Pie

This super-easy pie even makes its own crust!

2 cups cut-up cooked turkey
1 jar (4½ ounces) sliced mushrooms, drained
½ cup sliced green onions (with tops)
½ teaspoon salt
1 cup shredded Swiss cheese (4 ounces)
¾ cup Bisquick® Original baking mix
1½ cups milk
3 eggs

Heat oven to 400°. Grease pie plate, 10 × 1½ inches, lightly. Sprinkle turkey, mushrooms, onions, salt and cheese in pie plate. Beat remaining ingredients 15 seconds in blender on high speed or 1 minute with hand beater or until smooth. Pour into pie plate.

Bake 30 to 35 minutes or until golden brown and knife inserted halfway between center and edge comes out clean. Let stand 5 minutes before cutting. Refrigerate any remaining pie.

6 servings

PER SERVING: Calories 285; Protein 25 g; Carbohydrate 14 g; Fat 14 g; Cholesterol 200 mg; Sodium 500 mg

Turkey-Leek Casserole

Wash leeks several times in cold water to be sure all dirt has been removed.

5 medium leeks or 2 medium onions, sliced
2 tablespoons margarine or butter
2 tablespoons all-purpose flour
½ teaspoon salt
¼ teaspoon ground nutmeg
⅛ teaspoon pepper
1 cup chicken broth
1 cup milk
3 cups cut-up cooked turkey
½ cup finely chopped fully cooked smoked ham
1 jar (2 ounces) diced pimientos, drained
3 cups hot cooked noodles
1 cup shredded Swiss cheese (4 ounces)

Heat oven to 350°. Cook and stir leeks in margarine in 3-quart saucepan over medium heat about 5 minutes or until tender. Stir in flour, salt, nutmeg and pepper until blended. Cook over low heat, stirring constantly, until bubbly; remove from heat. Stir in broth and milk. Heat to boiling, stirring constantly. Boil and stir 1 minute. Stir in turkey, ham and pimientos.

Spread about half of the turkey mixture in ungreased square pan, 9 × 9 × 2 inches, or 2½-quart casserole. Spoon noodles over turkey mixture. Top with remaining turkey mixture. Sprinkle with cheese. Bake uncovered 25 to 30 minutes or until cheese is light brown. **8 servings**

PER SERVING: Calories 295; Protein 26 g; Carbohydrate 22 g; Fat 11 g; Cholesterol 60 mg; Sodium 480 mg

Turkey with Peppers

2 fresh turkey thighs (about 2 pounds)
2 tablespoons margarine or butter
1 tablespoon vegetable oil
½ cup water
2 tablespoons soy sauce
2 tablespoons chopped fresh parsley
½ teaspoon dried thyme leaves
¼ teaspoon dried rosemary leaves
2 medium green bell peppers, cut into ¼-inch strips
¼ cup sliced green onions (with tops)
1 teaspoon cornstarch
1 tablespoon cold water
2 tablespoons grated Parmesan cheese

Remove skin and bones from turkey; cut turkey into 2 × 1-inch strips. Cook turkey in margarine and oil in 10-inch skillet about 6 minutes, stirring occasionally, until light brown. Stir in ½ cup water, the soy sauce, parsley, thyme and rosemary. Heat to boiling; reduce heat. Cover and simmer about 30 minutes or until turkey is tender.

Stir in bell peppers and onions. Cover and simmer about 5 minutes or just until bell peppers are crisp-tender. Mix cornstarch and 1 tablespoon cold water; stir into turkey mixture. Heat to boiling, stirring constantly. Boil and stir 1 minute. Sprinkle with Parmesan cheese.

6 servings

PER SERVING: Calories 290; Protein 27 g; Carbohydrate 5 g; Fat 18 g; Cholesterol 85 mg; Sodium 490 mg

Savory Turkey Loaf

1¼ pounds fresh ground turkey
¾ cup fine dry bread crumbs
½ cup finely chopped onion (about
1 medium)
¾ cup milk
2 eggs, beaten
1 tablespoon Worcestershire sauce
1 tablespoon prepared horseradish
1 teaspoon poultry seasoning
1 teaspoon dry mustard
¼ teaspoon garlic powder
Salt and pepper to taste

Heat oven to 350°. Grease loaf pan, 8½ × 4½ × 2½ inches. Mix all ingredients in large bowl. Press mixture firmly in loaf pan. Bake about 1¼ hours or until turkey is no longer pink and mixture is firm. Let stand 10 minutes. Top each serving with ketchup if desired. **5 servings**

PER SERVING: Calories 310; Protein 26 g; Carbohydrate 16 g; Fat 15 g; Cholesterol 190 mg; Sodium 630 mg

French Omelet

Follow the line drawings below for perfect omelets.

2 teaspoons margarine or butter
2 eggs, beaten

Heat margarine in 8-inch omelet pan or skillet over medium-high heat just until margarine begins to brown. As margarine melts, tilt pan to coat bottom.

Quickly pour eggs into pan. Slide pan back and forth rapidly over heat and, at the same time, quickly stir with fork to spread eggs continuously over bottom of pan as they thicken. Let stand over heat a few seconds to brown bottom of omelet lightly. (Do not overcook—omelet will continue to cook after folding.)

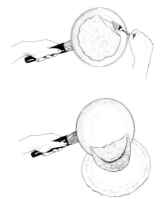

Tilt pan and run fork under edge of omelet, then jerk pan sharply to loosen from bottom of pan. Fold portion of omelet nearest you just to center. (Allow for portion of omelet to slide up side of pan.) Turn omelet onto warm plate, flipping folded portion of omelet over so far side is on bottom. Tuck sides of omelet under if necessary. **1 serving**

PER OMELET: Calories 225; Protein 18 g; Carbohydrate 1 g; Fat 19 g; Cholesterol 550 mg; Sodium 225 mg

Vegetable Frittata

A frittata is an Italian open-face omelet. It is not folded like a French omelet.

3 tablespoons vegetable oil
½ cup sliced zucchini
1 small bell pepper, cut into ¼-inch strips
1 small onion, thinly sliced
1 clove garlic, finely chopped
½ cup coarsely chopped tomato
2 teaspoons chopped fresh or ½ teaspoon dried oregano leaves
2 teaspoons chopped fresh or ½ teaspoon dried basil leaves
8 eggs
½ teaspoon salt
¼ teaspoon pepper
½ cup shredded Fontina or mozzarella cheese (2 ounces)
2 tablespoons grated Romano or Parmesan cheese

Heat oil in 10-inch ovenproof skillet over medium heat. Cook zucchini, bell pepper, onion and garlic in oil 3 minutes, stirring occasionally. Stir in tomato, oregano and basil. Reduce heat to medium-low. Beat eggs, salt and pepper until blended. Stir in Fontina cheese. Pour over vegetable mixture. Cover and cook 9 to 11 minutes or until eggs are set around edge and light brown on bottom. Sprinkle with Romano cheese.

Set oven control to broil. Broil frittata with top about 5 inches from heat about 3 minutes or until golden brown. **6 servings**

PER SERVING: Calories 215; Protein 11 g; Carbohydrate 5 g; Fat 17 g; Cholesterol 375 mg; Sodium 10 mg

Apple-Cheese Oven Pancake

Have the apple filling ready as soon as the pancake is done. You have to work quickly, or the pancake will deflate before you can place the filling on it.

1 cup all-purpose flour
1 cup skim milk
¼ teaspoon salt
2 eggs
4 egg whites
1 tablespoon margarine
2 cups thinly sliced unpared tart cooking apples (about 2 medium)
2 tablespoons chopped fresh or 2 teaspoons dried chives
2 tablespoons sugar
¼ cup shredded low-fat Cheddar cheese (1 ounce)

Heat oven to 450°. Spray rectangular baking dish, 13 × 9 × 2 inches, with nonstick cooking spray. Beat flour, milk, salt, eggs and egg whites until smooth; pour into dish. Bake about 15 to 20 minutes or until puffy and golden brown.

Meanwhile, heat margarine in 10-inch nonstick skillet over medium-high heat. Sauté apples and chives in margarine. Stir in sugar. Spoon apple mixture onto pancake. Sprinkle with cheese. Bake about 1 minute or until cheese is melted. **4 servings**

PER SERVING: Calories 295; Protein 14 g; Carbohydrate 43 g; Fat 7 g; Cholesterol 105 mg; Sodium 340 mg

Apple-Cheese Oven Pancake

Tex-Mex Egg Salad

This very special egg salad turns the ho-hum into the highly delicious!

4 hard-cooked eggs, chopped
¼ cup reduced-calorie mayonnaise or salad dressing
¼ cup low-fat sour cream
¼ cup diced Monterey Jack cheese (1 ounce)
2 tablespoons chopped green onion (with top)
2 teaspoons chopped fresh cilantro or parsley
¼ teaspoon salt
1 jalapeño chili, seeded and finely chopped
4 medium tomatoes

Mix all ingredients except tomatoes. Cut stem ends from tomatoes. Place tomatoes cut sides down. Cut into sixths to within ½ inch of bottom. Carefully spread out sections. Spoon about ½ cup salad into each tomato. **4 servings**

PER SERVING: Calories 205; Protein 10 g; Carbohydrate 9 g; Fat 14 g; Cholesterol 235 mg; Sodium 380 mg

Mushroom and Leek Quiche

1½ cups hot cooked rice
1 egg white or 2 tablespoons cholesterol-free egg product
1 cup coarsely chopped fresh mushrooms (about 4 ounces)
1 cup thinly sliced leek (about 1 small)
½ cup shredded low-fat Swiss cheese (2 ounces)
⅔ cup mashed soft tofu
⅔ cup skim milk
¼ teaspoon salt
⅛ teaspoon ground nutmeg
5 eggs whites or ¾ cup cholesterol-free egg product
4 drops red pepper sauce
2 drops yellow food color*

Heat oven to 350°. Spray quiche dish or pie plate, 9 × 1¼ inches, with nonstick cooking spray. Mix rice and 1 egg white. Spread evenly on bottom and side of pie plate, covering plate completely, using rubber spatula. Bake uncovered 5 minutes.

Increase oven temperature to 425°. Spray 10-inch nonstick skillet with nonstick cooking spray. Heat over medium heat. Cook mushrooms and leek in skillet 3 minutes, stirring occasionally, until tender. Place in pie plate. Sprinkle with cheese. Place remaining ingredients in blender or food processor. Cover and blend or process until smooth. Pour over cheese. Bake 15 minutes.

Reduce oven temperature to 325°. Bake 20 to 25 minutes or until knife inserted halfway between center and edge comes out clean. Let stand 10 minutes before cutting.

6 servings

PER SLICE: Calories 165; Protein 14 g; Carbohydrate 19 g; Fat 3 g; Cholesterol 10 mg; Sodium 420 mg

If using cholesterol-free egg product, omit food color.

Three-Cheese Pie

1 cup shredded Cheddar cheese
(4 ounces)
1 cup shredded mozzarella cheese
(4 ounces)
1 cup shredded Monterey Jack cheese
(4 ounces)
½ cup chopped onion (about 1 medium)
2 tablespoons all-purpose flour
4 eggs
1 cup skim milk
½ teaspoon salt
½ teaspoon dry mustard
½ teaspoon Worcestershire sauce
2 medium tomatoes, sliced

Heat oven to 350°. Grease pie plate, 10 × 1½ inches, or quiche dish, 9 × 1½ inches. Mix cheeses, onion and flour. Spread in pie plate. Beat eggs slightly in large bowl. Beat in milk, salt, mustard and Worcestershire sauce. Pour over cheese mixture. Bake uncovered 35 to 40 minutes or until set. Let stand 10 minutes. Arrange tomato slices, overlapping slightly, around edge of pie.   **8 servings**

PER SERVING: Calories 225; Protein 15 g; Carbohydrate 7 g; Fat 15 g; Cholesterol 145 mg; Sodium 430 mg

Lentil and Brown Rice Soup

¾ cup dried lentils
½ cup uncooked brown or regular rice
6 cups water
½ teaspoon ground cumin
½ teaspoon salt
¼ teaspoon pepper
½ package (2.5-ounce size) onion soup mix (1 envelope)
3 ounces spinach, cut into ½-inch strips (about 1 cup)
2 tablespoons snipped cilantro or parsley
3 tablespoons lemon juice

Heat lentils, rice, water, cumin, salt, pepper and soup mix (dry) to boiling in 4-quart Dutch oven; reduce heat. Cover and simmer, stirring occasionally, until lentils are tender, about 40 minutes.

Stir in spinach, cilantro and lemon juice until spinach is wilted. Serve with additional snipped cilantro and lemon slices if desired.

4 servings

PER SERVING: Calories 250; Protein 13 g; Carbohydrate 45 g; Fat 2 g; Cholesterol 450 mg; Sodium 1080 mg

Winter Squash Soufflé

Winter Squash Soufflé

¼ **cup chopped onion (about 1 small)**
2 **tablespoons reduced-calorie margarine**
2 **tablespoons all-purpose flour**
¼ **teaspoon salt**
¼ **teaspoon ground nutmeg**
⅛ **teaspoon pepper**
1 **cup skim milk**
3 **eggs, separated**
1 **package (12 ounces) frozen squash, thawed**
2 **egg whites**
½ **teaspoon cream of tartar**
2 **tablespoons grated Parmesan cheese**

Heat oven to 350°. Make a 4-inch band of triple-thickness aluminum foil 2 inches longer than circumference of 6-cup soufflé dish or 1½-quart casserole; secure foil band around top edge of dish. Spray inside of dish and foil with nonstick cooking spray.

Cook onion in margarine in 2-quart nonstick saucepan until onion is softened. Stir in flour, salt, nutmeg and pepper. Cook over low heat, stirring constantly, until margarine is absorbed; remove from heat. Beat milk and egg yolks; stir into flour mixture. Heat to boiling, stirring constantly. Boil and stir 1 minute. Stir in squash.

Beat egg whites and cream of tartar in medium bowl on high speed until stiff but not dry. Stir about one-fourth of the egg white mixture into squash mixture. Fold squash mixture into remaining egg white mixture.

Carefully pour into soufflé dish. Bake uncovered about 50 minutes or until set and cracks feel dry when touched lightly. Carefully remove foil band and divide soufflé into 4 servings with 2 forks. Sprinkle each serving with Parmesan cheese. Serve immediately. **4 servings**

PER SERVING: Calories 195; Protein 11 g; Carbohydrate 17 g; Fat 9 g; Cholesterol 165 mg; Sodium 330 mg

Tomato Vegetable Soup with Yogurt

Try the cold variation for an easy summer meal.

1 **can (24 ounces) tomato juice (3 cups)**
¼ **to ½ teaspoon ground red pepper (cayenne)**
¼ **teaspoon salt**
1 **package (10 ounces) frozen whole kernel corn**
1 **bunch green onions (about 6 with tops), sliced**
1 **medium red or green bell pepper, coarsely chopped**
1 **medium zucchini, coarsely chopped**
1 **container (18 ounces) plain yogurt**

Heat all ingredients except yogurt to boiling in 4-quart Dutch oven; reduce heat. Simmer uncovered, stirring occasionally, until vegetables are crisp-tender, 7 to 8 minutes. Remove from heat; cool 5 minutes before adding yogurt to prevent curdling.

Stir yogurt into soup until smooth. Heat over medium heat, stirring constantly, just until hot (do not boil). Garnish with snipped cilantro or parsley if desired. **4 or 5 servings**

PER SERVING: Calories 200; Protein 11 g; Carbohydrate 34 g; Fat 2 g; Cholesterol 10 mg; Sodium 850 mg

COLD TOMATO VEGETABLE SOUP WITH YOGURT: After stirring in yogurt, cover and refrigerate soup until chilled. Garnish with alfalfa sprouts if desired.

Confetti Corned Beef Hash

4
Satisfying Meat Main Dishes

Confetti Corned Beef Hash

A delicious way to use leftover baked potatoes.

2 tablespoons reduced-calorie margarine
2 cups chopped cooked potatoes (about 2 medium)
1½ cups cut-up cooked corned beef or lean cooked beef (about 8 ounces)
½ cup chopped bell pepper (about 1 small)
¼ cup sliced green onions (with tops)
2 tablespoons chopped fresh parsley
1 teaspoon chopped fresh or ¼ teaspoon dried thyme leaves
2 hard-cooked eggs, chopped

Heat margarine in 10-inch nonstick skillet over medium heat. Stir in remaining ingredients. Cook uncovered 8 to 10 minutes, turning frequently, until hot. **4 servings**

> PER SERVING: Calories 270; Protein 15 g; Carbohydrate 12 g; Fat 17 g; Cholesterol 160 mg; Sodium 710 mg

Mushroom Minute Steaks

6 beef cubed steaks (about 2 pounds)
1 teaspoon salt
¼ teaspoon lemon pepper
½ cup dry white or red wine or beef broth
1 medium green bell pepper, chopped (about 1 cup)
1 small onion, chopped (about ¼ cup)
2 cans (4 ounces each) sliced mushrooms, undrained

Sprinkle beef steaks with salt and lemon pepper. Cook a few steaks at a time in 10-inch skillet over medium heat until brown, 5 to 10 minutes on each side.

Return steaks to skillet. Add wine, bell pepper, onion and mushrooms. Heat over low heat until mushrooms are hot, about 5 minutes. **6 servings**

> PER SERVING: Calories 250; Protein 32 g; Carbohydrate 3 g; Fat 10 g; Cholesterol 80 mg; Sodium 550 mg

Swiss Steak

3 tablespoons all-purpose flour
1 teaspoon dry mustard
½ teaspoon salt
Beef boneless round, tip or chuck steak,
    about ¾ inch thick (about 1½ pounds)
2 tablespoons vegetable oil
1 can (16 ounces) whole tomatoes,
    undrained
2 cloves garlic, finely chopped
1 cup water
1 large onion, sliced
1 large green bell pepper, sliced

Mix flour, mustard and salt. Sprinkle one side of beef steak with half of the flour mixture; pound in. Turn beef and pound in remaining flour mixture. Cut into 6 serving pieces.

Heat oil in 10-inch skillet until hot. Cook beef in oil over medium heat, turning once, until brown, about 15 minutes. Add tomatoes and garlic; break up tomatoes. Heat to boiling; reduce heat. Cover and simmer until beef is tender, about 1¼ hours. Add water, onion and bell pepper. Heat to boiling; reduce heat. Cover and simmer until vegetables are tender, 5 to 8 minutes. **6 servings**

PER SERVING: Calories 220; Protein 25 g; Carbohydrate 10 g; Fat 9 g; Cholesterol 60 mg; Sodium 350 mg

Crushed Pepper–Beef Kabobs

1 pound beef boneless round, tip or
    chuck steak
½ cup dry red wine
1 tablespoon olive or vegetable oil
½ teaspoon salt
1 clove garlic, cut in half
2 tablespoons prepared mustard
2 tablespoons black peppercorns,
    coarsely crushed
2 small onions, cut lengthwise into
    fourths
2 small zucchini, cut into 1-inch slices
1 red or yellow bell pepper, cut into
    1-inch pieces
4 mushrooms
Olive oil

Trim excess fat from beef steak; cut beef into 1-inch cubes. Place in glass or plastic bowl. Mix wine, 1 tablespoon oil, the salt and garlic; pour over beef. Cover and refrigerate at least 6 hours but no longer than 24 hours, stirring occasionally.

Remove beef; drain thoroughly. Thread beef cubes on four 11-inch metal skewers, leaving space between cubes. Brush with mustard; sprinkle with peppercorns.

Set oven control to broil. Place kabobs on rack in broiler pan. Broil with tops about 3 inches from heat 5 minutes; turn. Broil 5 minutes longer.

Alternate onion, zucchini and bell pepper on each of four 11-inch metal skewers, leaving space between each. Top each with mushroom. Place kabobs on rack in broiler pan with beef. Turn beef; brush vegetables with oil. Broil kabobs 5 to 6 minutes, turning and brushing vegetables with oil, until beef is done and vegetables are crisp-tender. **4 servings**

PER SERVING: Calories 315; Protein 24 g; Carbohydrate 8 g; Fat 19 g; Cholesterol 70 mg; Sodium 430 mg

Beef Medallions with Rosemary Sauce

1-pound beef tenderloin, about 6 inches long
1 tablespoon margarine or butter
1 tablespoon margarine or butter
½ teaspoon cocoa
⅛ teaspoon salt
1 clove garlic, finely chopped
1 teaspoon chopped fresh or ¼ teaspoon dried rosemary leaves
¼ cup dry red wine or beef broth

Cut beef tenderloin into ¾-inch slices. Heat 1 tablespoon margarine in 10-inch skillet over medium-high heat. Sauté beef in margarine over medium-high heat 4 to 5 minutes on each side, turning once, until brown and center is medium rare. Remove beef to warm platter; keep warm.

Cook and stir 1 tablespoon margarine, the cocoa, salt, garlic and rosemary in same skillet until bubbly. Gradually stir in wine. Heat to boiling; boil and stir 1 minute. Serve over beef.

4 servings

PER SERVING: Calories 235; Protein 23 g; Carbohydrate 1 g; Fat 14 g; Cholesterol 70 mg; Sodium 125 mg

PORK MEDALLIONS WITH ROSEMARY SAUCE: Substitute 1-pound pork tenderloin for the beef and dry white or rosé wine for the dry red wine. Sauté pork about 6 minutes on each side or until done.

Fat-Slashing Tips

If you love sour cream, as well as mayonnaise, salad dressing or flavored yogurt, try the following tips to reduce calories.

• You can purchase a wide selection of high-quality reduced-calorie, low-fat and nonfat products at your supermarket. Calories can be reduced even further if the reduced-calorie versions of these foods are mixed with equal parts of nonfat plain yogurt. You'll cut calories without losing taste!

• To control calories in flavored yogurts, mix your own. Purchase nonfat plain yogurt and flavor it yourself by adding artificial sweetener, vanilla, cut-up or mashed fresh fruit, sugar-free fruit preserves, fruit juice concentrate, instant fruit drink mix or instant coffee. Eat yogurt plain, with a muffin, over cereal, as a main dish salad dressing, with fresh fruit or on top of angel food cake. It's versatile and healthful, and will satisfy the desire for something creamy and filling.

Spicy Stir-fried Beef

1½ pounds boneless beef sirloin steak
1 tablespoon cornstarch
1 tablespoon vegetable oil
1 tablespoon soy sauce
1 teaspoon sugar
¼ teaspoon pepper
1 tablespoon soy sauce
¼ to ½ teaspoon crushed red pepper
2 tablespoons vegetable oil
1 teaspoon finely chopped gingerroot
2 large cloves garlic, finely chopped
1 large green bell pepper, cut into ¼-inch
   strips
2 medium carrots, shredded (about
   1 cup)
1 can (8 ounces) bamboo shoots, drained
1 can (8 ounces) sliced water chestnuts,
   drained
4 green onions (with tops), cut into
   2-inch pieces

Trim fat from beef. Cut beef into 2-inch-wide strips. Cut strips into ⅛-inch slices. Stack slices and cut into thin strips. (Beef is easier to slice if partially frozen.) Toss beef, cornstarch, 1 table-spoon oil, 1 tablespoon soy sauce, the sugar and pepper in glass or plastic bowl. Cover and refrigerate 30 minutes. Mix 1 tablespoon soy sauce and the red pepper; let stand at room temperature.

Heat 2 tablespoons oil in 12-inch skillet or wok over high heat until hot. Add beef mixture, gingerroot and garlic; cook and stir until beef is brown, about 5 minutes. Add bell pepper, carrots, bamboo shoots and water chestnuts; cook and stir 3 minutes. Add onions and red pepper mixture; cook and stir 1 minute.

6 servings

PER SERVING: Calories 235; Protein 23 g; Carbohy-drate 13 g; Fat 10 g; Cholesterol 55 mg; Sodium 400 mg

Beef Stroganoff

The wonderful taste of this classic dish—without all the calories!

1 pound lean beef boneless round steak,
   about ½ inch thick
1 tablespoon reduced-calorie margarine
½ cup chopped onion (about 1 medium)
1 clove garlic, finely chopped
3 cups sliced mushrooms (about
   8 ounces)
¼ cup dry red wine or beef broth
2 tablespoons cornstarch
1 cup condensed beef broth
¼ teaspoon pepper
¾ cup nonfat plain yogurt
2 cups hot cooked noodles or rice
2 tablespoons snipped parsley

Trim fat from beef steak; cut beef with grain into 2-inch strips. Cut strips diagonally across grain into ¼-inch slices. (For ease in cutting, partially freeze beef, about 1½ hours.) Heat margarine in 10-inch nonstick skillet until melted. Add onion and garlic; cook and stir over medium-high heat until onion is tender. Stir in beef and mush-rooms; cook and stir until beef is no longer pink. Stir in wine; reduce heat. Cover and simmer 10 minutes.

Stir cornstarch into beef broth until dissolved; stir into beef mixture. Cook and stir over medium-high heat until thickened; remove from heat. Stir in pepper and yogurt; reduce heat. Cover and simmer, stirring occasionally, until beef is tender, about 30 minutes. Serve over noodles; sprinkle with parsley.

6 servings

PER SERVING: Calories 230; Protein 22 g; Carbohy-drate 21 g; Fat 6 g; Cholesterol 65 mg; Sodium 330 mg

Indian Beef with Cucumber Rice

1½ **pounds lean beef boneless chuck roast**
1 **cup nonfat plain yogurt**
1 **teaspoon cardamom seeds (removed from pods), crushed**
¼ **teaspoon ground cloves**
⅛ **teaspoon ground nutmeg**
1 **tablespoon reduced-calorie margarine**
2 **cups chopped onions (about 2 large)**
1 **tablespoon grated gingerroot**
2 **cloves garlic, finely chopped**
¾ **teaspoon coriander seed, crushed**
½ **teaspoon cumin seed**
¼ **teaspoon ground turmeric**
¾ **teaspoon salt**
Cucumber Rice (below)
¼ **cup cold water**
1 **tablespoon cornstarch**
1 **tablespoon all-purpose flour**
¼ **cup nonfat plain yogurt**
Snipped fresh cilantro

Trim fat from beef roast; cut beef into 1-inch cubes. Mix 1 cup yogurt, the cardamom, cloves and nutmeg in glass or plastic bowl or heavy plastic bag; stir in beef. Cover and refrigerate at least 4 hours.

Heat margarine in 10-inch nonstick skillet over medium heat until melted. Cook and stir onions, gingerroot and garlic about 2 minutes. Stir in beef mixture, coriander, cumin, turmeric and salt. Heat to boiling; reduce heat. Cover and cook, stirring occasionally, until meat is tender, about 1½ hours.

Prepare Cucumber Rice. Shake water, cornstarch and flour in tightly covered container; gradually stir into beef mixture. Heat to boiling, stirring constantly. Boil and stir 1 minute. Serve beef mixture over Cucumber Rice; drizzle with yogurt and sprinkle with cilantro.

6 servings

PER SERVING: Calories 330; Protein 32 g; Carbohydrate 28 g; Fat 10 g; Cholesterol 85 mg; Sodium 650 mg

Cucumber Rice

2 **cups hot cooked rice**
1 **cup chopped seeded cucumber (about 1 medium)**
2 **tablespoons lemon juice**

Mix all ingredients; heat if necessary.

Beef Teriyaki

1 **pound beef boneless sirloin steak**
¼ **cup soy sauce**
¼ **cup dry sherry, white wine or chicken broth**
1 **tablespoon vegetable oil**
2 **teaspoons chopped gingerroot or** ½ **teaspoon ground ginger**
1 **teaspoon sugar**
1 **clove garlic, chopped**

Trim fat from beef steak; cut beef into ¾-inch cubes. Place beef in glass or plastic bowl. Mix remaining ingredients; pour over beef. Cover and refrigerate, stirring occasionally, at least 1 hour.

Thread 6 beef cubes on each of 5 skewers; brush with marinade. Set oven control to broil. Broil kabobs with tops about 4 inches from heat 5 to 6 minutes; turn. Brush with marinade; broil until done, 5 to 6 minutes longer. Brush with marinade.

5 servings

PER SERVING: Calories 100; Protein 17 g; Carbohydrate 1 g; Fat 3 g; Cholesterol 45 g; Sodium 240 mg

Beef-Vegetable Stew with Barley

Beef-Vegetable Stew with Barley

1 pound beef stew meat, cut into 1-inch pieces
1 tablespoon vegetable oil
1 cup dry red wine or beef broth
1 teaspoon chopped fresh or ¼ teaspoon dried rosemary leaves, crushed
¼ teaspoon pepper
1 clove garlic, finely chopped
1 can (10½ ounces) condensed beef broth
1 can (14½ ounces) whole tomatoes, undrained
½ cup uncooked barley
1 cup broccoli flowerets
2 cups sliced carrots (about 2 medium)
1 medium onion, cut into wedges
4 ounces medium mushrooms, cut into halves

Cook beef in oil in 4-quart Dutch oven, stirring occasionally, until brown. Stir in wine, rosemary, pepper, garlic, broth and tomatoes; break up tomatoes. Heat to boiling; reduce heat. Cover and simmer 1 hour.

Stir in barley. Cover and simmer about 30 minutes or until beef is almost tender. Stir in remaining ingredients. Cover and simmer about 20 minutes or until vegetables are tender.

4 servings

PER SERVING: Calories 290; Protein 23 g; Carbohydrate 23 g; Fat 9 g; Cholesterol 55 mg; Sodium 330 mg

Vegetable-Beef Burgers

1½ pounds ground beef
1 cup bean sprouts, coarsely chopped
¼ cup chopped green bell pepper
1 small onion, chopped (about ¼ cup)
1 small carrot, shredded (about ¼ cup)
1 small stalk celery, chopped (about ¼ cup)
½ teaspoon salt
¼ teaspoon pepper
1½ cups alfalfa sprouts
2 medium tomatoes, each cut into 3 slices

Mix ground beef, bean sprouts, bell pepper, onion, carrot, celery, salt and pepper. Shape beef mixture into 6 patties, each about ½ inch thick. Place patties on rack in broiler pan.

Set oven control to broil. Broil patties with tops about 3 inches from heat until medium doneness, 3 to 5 minutes on each side. Top each patty with ¼ cup alfalfa sprouts and 1 tomato slice.

6 servings

PER SERVING: Calories 245; Protein 25 g; Carbohydrate 5 g; Fat 14 g; Cholesterol 70 mg; Sodium 240 mg

Sauerbraten Meatballs and Noodles

Sauerbraten Meatballs and Noodles

1 pound lean ground beef or pork
1/3 cup crushed gingersnaps (about
  6 gingersnaps)
1/2 cup finely chopped onion (about
  1 medium)
1/4 cup water
1/2 teaspoon salt
1/4 teaspoon pepper
6 ounces uncooked egg noodles or
  spaetzle (about 3 cups)
1 cup beef broth
1/4 cup apple cider vinegar
1 tablespoon sugar
1/4 cup crushed gingersnaps (about
  4 gingersnaps)
2 tablespoons raisins

Heat oven to 400°. Mix ground beef, 1/3 cup gingersnaps, the onion, water, salt and pepper. Shape mixture into 24 meatballs. Spray rack in broiler pan with nonstick cooking spray. Place meatballs on rack. Bake uncovered 20 to 25 minutes or until done and light brown.

Cook noodles as directed on package; drain. Mix remaining ingredients except raisins in 1 1/2-quart saucepan. Cook over medium heat, stirring constantly, until mixture thickens and boils. Stir in raisins and meatballs. Heat until hot. Serve over noodles. **6 servings**

PER SERVING: Calories 300; Protein 24 g; Carbohydrate 34 g; Fat 7 g; Cholesterol 85 mg; Sodium 480 mg

Beef and Artichoke Fettuccine

8 ounces uncooked fettuccine
1 jar (6 ounces) marinated artichoke
  hearts, cut into halves and marinade
  reserved
1 small onion, finely chopped (about
  1/4 cup)
1 cup half-and-half
1/2 cup grated Parmesan cheese
2 cups julienne strips cooked roast beef
  (about 8 ounces)
Freshly ground pepper
1/3 cup chopped toasted pecans

Cook fettuccine as directed on package. While fettuccine is cooking, heat reserved artichoke marinade in 10-inch skillet over medium heat. Cook onion in marinade about 4 minutes, stirring occasionally. Stir in half-and-half; heat until hot. Stir in Parmesan cheese, artichoke hearts and beef. Heat until hot.

Drain fettuccine; stir into sauce and toss with 2 forks. Sprinkle with pepper and pecans.

6 servings

PER SERVING: Calories 320; Protein 20 g; Carbohydrate 28 g; Fat 14 g; Cholesterol 55 mg; Sodium 190 mg

Pork and Broccoli Risotto

1 pound pork boneless loin or leg
2 teaspoons vegetable oil
3 cups broccoli flowerets
1 medium red bell pepper, chopped
  (about 1 cup)
2 cloves garlic, finely chopped
1 teaspoon salt
1 tablespoon margarine or butter
1 medium onion, chopped (about ½ cup)
1 cup uncooked regular long grain rice
¼ cup dry white wine or beef broth
1 cup beef broth
1¼ cups water
¼ cup milk
2 tablespoons grated Parmesan cheese

Trim fat from pork loin. Cut pork into slices, 2 ×
1 × ¼ inch. (For ease in cutting, partially freeze
pork about 1 hour.) Heat oil in 10-inch skillet
over medium-high heat. Sauté pork, broccoli,
bell pepper, garlic and salt in oil about 4 minutes
or until pork is no longer pink and vegetables are
crisp-tender. Remove from skillet; keep warm.

Heat margarine in same skillet over medium
heat. Cook onion about 3 minutes. Stir in rice
and wine. Cook and stir about 30 seconds or
until wine is absorbed. Stir in broth and water.
Heat to boiling; reduce heat. Cover and simmer
about 15 minutes, stirring occasionally, or until
rice is almost tender and mixture is creamy. Stir
in milk and pork mixture; heat until hot. Sprinkle
with Parmesan cheese.   **6 servings**

PER SERVING: Calories 230; Protein 13 g; Carbohydrate 5 g; Fat 15 g; Cholesterol 45 mg; Sodium 650 mg

Pork and Tofu Stir-fry

*Tofu, the curd made from soybeans, has the
most protein for its calories of all legume
products. Without an assertive flavor of its
own, it is a nice carrier for seasonings and
sauces, and can be used alone or to extend
meats.*

½ pound lean pork boneless loin or leg
1 teaspoon cornstarch
1 teaspoon low-sodium soy sauce
1 cup Chinese pea pods (about
  3½ ounces)
2 teaspoons vegetable oil
1 teaspoon finely chopped gingerroot or
  ½ teaspoon ground ginger
1 clove garlic, finely chopped
1 cup sliced fresh mushrooms (about
  3 ounces)
¼ cup sliced green onions (with tops)
2 teaspoons oyster sauce
1 teaspoon low-sodium soy sauce
5 ounces firm tofu, cut into ½-inch cubes

Trim fat from pork loin. Cut pork into 2 × 1 ×
⅛-inch slices. (For ease in cutting, partially
freeze pork about 1½ hours.) Toss pork, cornstarch and 1 teaspoon soy sauce in medium
glass or plastic bowl. Cover and refrigerate 20
minutes. Heat 1 inch water to boiling in 1½-quart
saucepan. Add pea pods. Cover and boil 1 minute; drain. Immediately rinse with cold water;
drain.

Heat oil in 10-inch nonstick skillet or wok over
high heat. Add pork mixture, gingerroot and garlic; stir-fry about 3 minutes or until pork is no
longer pink. Add mushrooms and onions; stir-fry
2 minutes longer. Add remaining ingredients;
stir-fry until heated through and mixed
thoroughly.   **4 servings**

PER SERVING: Calories 165; Protein 15 g; Carbohydrate 7 g; Fat 9 g; Cholesterol 35 mg; Sodium 130 mg

Pork and Tofu Stir-fry

Mayonnaise and Salad Dressing

Salads are great low-calorie meals, but not when served with high-fat dressings. Follow these tips to tame fat in salad dressings.

- Reduced-calorie, light or "lite" mayonnaise contains 20 to 50 calories per tablespoon.
- Regular, cholesterol-free mayonnaise and salad dressing has 60 to 100 calories per tablespoon but does not contain cholesterol because the egg yolk has been omitted.
- Reduced-calorie, light or "lite" cholesterol-free mayonnaise contains 20 to 50 calories per tablespoon and also has no cholesterol.
- Vinaigrette-type bottled salad dressings are made from vegetable oils and are cholesterol-free but can contain 45 to 100 calories and 4 to 9 grams of fat per tablespoon. The total oil content has been cut in the reduced-calorie counterparts, which in many cases are oil-free. Recipes for salad dressings typically use 3 parts oil to 1 part vinegar. Try using 1 part oil to 1 part vinegar. Mild vinegars with flavorings such as balsamic or raspberry reduce tartness.
- Creamy bottled salad dressings vary widely in fat content, cholesterol and calorie counts. Many bottled dressings average 60 to 80 calories and 6 to 8 grams of fat per tablespoon, while the reduced-calorie versions are one-quarter to one-half that amount.

Pork and Mango Salad

If you like, use skinless chicken instead of pork, and you'll save about 45 calories per serving.

1 large mango or papaya
1/2 cup plain nonfat yogurt
1 teaspoon sugar
1/4 teaspoon ground ginger
4 cups shredded Boston or iceberg lettuce
2 cups julienne strips cooked lean pork (about 8 ounces)
1 cup orange sections (about 2 medium)
1/2 avocado, peeled and thinly sliced

Cut mango in half and peel. Mash enough mango to measure 1/4 cup; cut remaining mango into thin slices. Mix mashed mango, yogurt, sugar and ginger.

Place 1 cup lettuce on each of 4 salad plates. Arrange mango slices, pork, oranges and avocado on lettuce. Top each salad with mango mixture. **4 servings**

PER SERVING: Calories 290; Protein 19 g; Carbohydrate 27 g; Fat 13 g; Cholesterol 50 mg; Sodium 70 mg

Pork and Mango Salad

Easy Cassoulet

This dish thickens as it stands, and you can thin it with a little wine if you wish. It's an excellent company dish, using kitchen staples, and can be made quickly on short notice.

1 pound Polish or smoked sausage, diagonally sliced into 1-inch pieces
1 can (15½ ounces) great northern beans, drained
1 can (15 ounces) kidney beans, drained
1 can (15 ounces) black beans, drained
1 can (15 ounces) tomato sauce
3 medium carrots, thinly sliced
2 small onions, thinly sliced and separated into rings
2 tablespoons packed brown sugar
½ cup dry red wine or beef broth
2 tablespoons chopped fresh or 1½ teaspoons dried thyme leaves
2 cloves garlic, finely chopped

Heat oven to 375°. Mix all ingredients in ungreased 3-quart casserole. Cover and bake 50 to 60 minutes or until hot and bubbly and carrots are tender.   **8 servings**

PER SERVING: Calories 260; Protein 18 g; Carbohydrate 35 g; Fat 5 g; Cholesterol 30 mg; Sodium 1260 mg

MICROWAVE DIRECTIONS: Place carrots and red wine in 3-quart microwavable casserole. Cover and microwave on high 5 minutes. Place sausage on carrots. Mix remaining ingredients. Pour over top. Cover tightly and microwave on high 18 to 22 minutes, stirring after 12 minutes, until hot and bubbly.

Lamb with Yogurt-Mint Sauce

⅔ cup plain nonfat yogurt
¼ cup firmly packed fresh mint leaves
2 tablespoons sugar
4 lamb loin chops, about 1 inch thick (about 1 pound)

Place yogurt, mint and sugar in blender or food processor. Cover and blend or process until smooth.

Set oven control to broil. Spray broiler pan rack with nonstick cooking spray. Trim fat from lamb chops. Place lamb on rack in broiler pan. Broil with tops 2 to 3 inches from heat 12 to 14 minutes, turning lamb after 6 minutes, until desired doneness. Serve with sauce.

4 servings

PER CHOP: Calories 255; Protein 34 g; Carbohydrate 9 g; Fat 9 g; Cholesterol 115 mg; Sodium 105 mg

Lamb with Yogurt-Mint Sauce

Lamb Shish Kabobs

1 pound lamb boneless shoulder
¼ cup lemon juice
2 tablespoons olive or vegetable oil
2 teaspoons salt
2 teaspoons chopped fresh or ½ teaspoon dried oregano leaves
¼ teaspoon pepper
1 green bell pepper, cut into 1-inch
   pieces
1 medium onion, cut into eighths
1 cup cubed eggplant

Trim excess fat from lamb shoulder. Cut lamb into 1-inch cubes. Place lamb in glass or plastic bowl. Mix lemon juice, oil, salt, oregano and pepper. Pour over lamb. Cover and refrigerate at least 6 hours, stirring occasionally. Remove lamb from marinade; reserve marinade.

Set oven control to broil. Thread lamb on four 11-inch metal skewers, leaving space between each. Broil with tops about 3 inches from heat 5 minutes; turn. Brush with reserved marinade. Broil 5 minutes longer.

Alternate bell pepper, onion and eggplant on each of four 11-inch metal skewers, leaving space between each piece. Place vegetables on rack in broiler pan with lamb. Turn lamb. Brush lamb and vegetables with marinade. Broil kabobs 4 to 5 minutes, turning and brushing twice with marinade, until brown.   **4 servings**

PER KABOB: Calories 235; Protein 24 g; Carbohydrate 6 g; Fat 13 g; Cholesterol 80 mg; Sodium 1150 mg

Greek Lamb and Orzo

Orzo is a type of pasta that resembles rice.

1 pound ground lamb
1 can (16 ounces) stewed tomatoes,
   undrained
1 stalk celery, cut into ½-inch pieces
½ cup orzo
½ teaspoon salt
¼ teaspoon ground red pepper (cayenne)
Plain yogurt

Cook and stir ground lamb in 10-inch skillet until lamb is light brown; drain. Stir in tomatoes, celery, orzo, salt and red pepper. Heat to boiling; reduce heat. Cover and simmer about 12 minutes, stirring frequently, until tomato liquid is absorbed and orzo is tender. Serve with yogurt.   **4 servings**

PER SERVING: Calories 285; Protein 24 g; Carbohydrate 7 g; Fat 17 g; Cholesterol 85 mg; Sodium 540 mg

MICROWAVE DIRECTIONS: Crumble ground lamb into 2-quart microwavable casserole. Cover with waxed paper and microwave on high 5 to 6 minutes, stirring after 3 minutes, until no longer pink; drain. Stir in remaining ingredients except yogurt. Cover tightly and microwave 12 to 14 minutes, stirring every 4 minutes, until orzo is tender. Serve with yogurt.

GREEK BEEF AND ORZO: Substitute 1 pound ground beef for the lamb.

5
Guilt-Free Desserts

Watermelon with Blackberries and Pear Puree

3 slices watermelon, ¾ inch thick each
1½ cups blackberries
Pear Puree (below)

Cut each watermelon slice into 10 wedges. Cut rind from wedges and remove seeds. Arrange wedges on 6 dessert plates. Top with blackberries. Refrigerate about 1 hour or until chilled. Top each serving with Pear Puree.

Pear Puree

2 medium pears
¼ cup light rum

Pare pears. Cut into fourths; remove cores and stems. Place pears and rum in blender or food processor. Cover and blend or process on medium about 1 minute or until smooth.

PER SERVING: Calories 100; Protein 1 g; Carbohydrate 18 g; Fat 1 g; Cholesterol 0 mg; Sodium 5 mg

Gingered Pineapple

1 medium pineapple, pared and cut into chunks*
1 teaspoon finely chopped gingerroot or ½ teaspoon ground ginger
1 medium orange

Sprinkle pineapple with gingerroot. Grate 2 teaspoons orange peel; sprinkle over pineapple. Cut orange in half and remove seeds. Squeeze juice (about ¼ cup) over pineapple. Stir gently. Cover and refrigerate at least 1 hour, stirring once, to blend flavors.   **6 servings**

PER SERVING: Calories 45; Protein 0 g; Carbohydrate 11 g; Fat 0 g; Cholesterol 0 mg; Sodium 0 mg

*3 cans (8 ounces each) pineapple chunks in juice, drained, can be substituted for the fresh pineapple.

Honeydew Sorbet with Strawberry Puree

A food processor makes preparing refreshing sorbets a snap. Try to select ripe (sweet) fruit, as there is no added sweetening.

½ **medium honeydew melon, pared and cut into 1-inch chunks**
2 **cups strawberries**
1 **teaspoon lemon juice**
6 **strawberries**

Place melon chunks in ungreased jelly roll pan, 15½ × 10½ × 1 inch. Cover and freeze until hard, at least 2 hours.

Place 2 cups strawberries in workbowl of food processor fitted with steel blade. Cover and process until smooth. Place about 3 tablespoons strawberry puree on each of 6 plates.

Wash workbowl and blade. Place half of the frozen melon chunks and ½ teaspoon lemon juice at a time in workbowl of food processor. Cover and process until smooth. Scoop or spoon about ½ cup melon mixture over strawberry puree. (Melon mixture may be frozen up to 30 minutes before serving.) Garnish with remaining strawberries and serve immediately. **6 servings**

PER SERVING: Calories 50; Protein 0 g; Carbohydrate 13 g; Fat 0 g; Cholesterol 0 mg; Sodium 10 mg

NOTE: If sorbet is to be frozen longer than 1 hour, remove from freezer about 45 minutes before serving.

Peach Sorbet with Pineapple

1 **package (16 ounces) frozen unsweetened peach slices**
¼ **cup unsweetened apple juice**
6 **slices pineapple, ½ inch thick***

Place half of the peaches and 2 tablespoons apple juice at a time in food processor. Cover and process until smooth. Freeze at least 2 hours or until icy. Scoop or spoon over pineapple slices. (If sorbet becomes too firm to scoop, remove from freezer about 1 hour before serving.) **6 servings**

PER SERVING: Calories 125; Protein 1 g; Carbohydrate 30 g; Fat 0 g; Cholesterol 0 mg; Sodium 5 mg

*6 canned pineapple slices in juice, drained, can be substituted for fresh pineapple slices.

Shopping Smart

- Never shop for groceries when you are hungry.
- Make out a grocery list before going to the store and stick to it.
- Limit "impulse" buying by treating yourself to fruits and vegetables, or such low-calorie treats as sesame rice cakes or reduced-calorie frozen desserts.
- Less time spent in the supermarket means less temptation to resist.
- Read food labels and know what it is you are paying for.
- If you don't buy it, you can't eat it.

Cranberry Ice

1 pound cranberries
2 cups water
2 cups sugar
¼ cup lemon juice
1 teaspoon grated orange peel
2 cups cold water

Cook cranberries in 2 cups water about 10 minutes or until skins are broken. Rub cranberries through sieve to make smooth pulp. Stir in sugar, lemon juice and orange peel. Stir in 2 cups cold water. Pour into square baking dish, 8 × 8 × 2 inches. Freeze, stirring several times to keep mixture smooth, until firm. Let stand at room temperature 10 minutes before serving. **8 servings**

PER SERVING: Calories 215; Protein 0 g; Carbohydrate 55 g; Fat 0 g; Cholesterol 0 mg; Sodium 5 mg

Baked Maple Apples

4 medium baking apples (Rome Beauty,
  Golden Delicious, Greening)
4 teaspoons margarine
¼ cup maple-flavored syrup

Heat oven to 375°. Core apples. Pare 1-inch strip of skin from around middle of each apple, or pare upper half of each to prevent splitting.

Place apples upright in ungreased square baking dish, 8 × 8 × 2 inches. Place 1 teaspoon margarine and 1 tablespoon maple-flavored syrup in center of each apple. Pour water (¼ inch deep) into baking dish.

Bake uncovered 30 to 40 minutes or until tender when pierced with fork. (Time will vary with size and variety of apple.) Spoon syrup in dish over apples several times during baking.

4 servings

PER SERVING: Calories 180; Protein 0 g; Carbohydrate 38 g; Fat 4 g; Cholesterol 0 mg; Sodium 75 mg

Blueberry-Lime Torte

Blueberry-Lime Torte

Fresh blueberries and lime cream are mounded in a crisp meringue shell.

Meringue Shell (right)
2 egg whites
1 egg
½ cup sugar
⅔ cup water
⅓ cup lime juice
1 envelope unflavored gelatin
1 tablespoon grated lime peel
4 egg whites
½ teaspoon cream of tartar
½ cup sugar
1½ cups blueberries

Bake Meringue Shell; cool completely. Beat 2 egg whites and the egg in medium bowl until foamy. Mix ½ cup sugar, the water, lime juice and gelatin in 2-quart nonstick saucepan. Heat to boiling over medium heat, stirring constantly. Gradually stir at least half of the hot mixture into egg mixture. Stir into hot mixture in saucepan. Heat to boiling; remove from heat. Stir in lime peel. Place pan in bowl of ice and water, or refrigerate about 15 minutes, stirring occasionally, until mixture mounds when dropped from spoon.

Beat 4 egg whites and the cream of tartar in large bowl until foamy. Beat in ½ cup sugar, 1 tablespoon at a time. Continue beating until stiff and glossy. Do not underbeat. Fold in lime mixture. Place blueberries in shell. Spoon lime mixture over blueberries. Refrigerate about 3 hours or until set. Garnish with lime twist and blueberries if desired. **8 servings**

PER SERVING: Calories 210; Protein 5 g; Carbohydrate 47 g; Fat 1 g; Cholesterol 25 mg; Sodium 70 mg

Meringue Shell

3 egg whites
¼ teaspoon cream of tartar
¾ cup sugar

Heat oven to 275°. Line cookie sheet with cooking parchment paper or aluminum foil. Beat egg whites and cream of tartar in medium bowl until foamy. Beat in sugar, 1 tablespoon at a time. Continue beating until stiff and glossy. Do not underbeat. Shape meringue on cookie sheet into 9-inch circle with back of spoon, building up side. Bake 1 hour. Turn off oven. Leave meringue in oven with door closed 1½ hours. Finish cooling meringue at room temperature.

Almond-Apple Crisp

1 tablespoon water
1 teaspoon almond extract
6 cups sliced unpared, tart eating apples
 (about 4 medium)
½ cup coarsely crushed zwieback
 crumbs
2 tablespoons all-purpose flour
2 tablespoons sugar
2 tablespoons chopped almonds
½ teaspoon ground cinnamon
3 tablespoons reduced-calorie margarine
Yogurt Topping (below)

Heat oven to 375°. Mix water and almond extract; toss with apples in 1½-quart casserole sprayed with nonstick cooking spray. Mix remaining ingredients except Yogurt Topping until crumbly; sprinkle over apples.

Bake until top is golden brown and apples are tender, about 30 minutes. Serve warm with Yogurt Topping. **6 servings**

PER SERVING: Calories 160; Protein 2 g; Carbohydrate 24 g; Fat 7 g; Cholesterol 0 mg; Sodium 80 mg

Yogurt Topping

½ cup nonfat plain yogurt
⅛ teaspoon almond extract
1 teaspoon sugar

Mix all ingredients.

MICROWAVE DIRECTIONS: Prepare as directed—except use microwavable pie plate, 9 × 1¼ inches. Microwave uncovered on high 5 minutes; rotate pie plate ½ turn. Microwave until apples are tender, 4 to 7 minutes longer.

Carrot Cake

Sugar and oil are significantly reduced as compared to traditional recipes.

1 can (8 ounces) crushed pineapple in
 juice, drained (reserve ¼ cup juice)
1 cup all-purpose flour
1 cup shredded carrots (about 2 small)
½ cup packed brown sugar
⅓ cup chopped walnuts
¼ cup vegetable oil
1 teaspoon vanilla
¾ teaspoon baking soda
½ teaspoon ground cinnamon
¼ teaspoon salt
¼ teaspoon ground cloves
¼ teaspoon ground ginger
1 egg
¾ cup thawed frozen whipped topping

Heat oven to 350°. Spray round pan, 8 × 1½ inches, with nonstick cooking spray. Reserve ¼ cup crushed pineapple. Blend ¼ cup of the crushed pineapple, the reserved juice and remaining ingredients except whipped topping in medium bowl on low speed, scraping bowl constantly, 1 minute. Beat on medium speed, scraping bowl occasionally, 2 minutes. Pour batter into pan. Bake until wooden pick inserted in center comes out clean, 25 to 35 minutes; cool. Fold remaining pineapple into topping until creamy; serve with cake. **8 slices**

PER SLICE WITH 2 TABLESPOONS TOPPING: Calories 220; Protein 3 g; Carbohydrate 26 g; Fat 12 g; Cholesterol 35 mg; Sodium 190 mg

MICROWAVE DIRECTIONS: Prepare as directed—except use round microwavable dish, 8 × 1½ inches. Microwave uncovered on medium (50%), rotating dish ¼ turn every 3 minutes, until surface is almost dry, 9 to 12 minutes. Let cool on heatproof surface (do not use rack.) Continue as directed.

Pumpkin Squares

Like miniature square pumpkin pies.

2 enveloped unflavored gelatin
¾ cup unsweetened apple juice
½ cup water
1 can (16 ounces) pumpkin
2 tablespoons packed brown sugar
½ teaspoon ground cinnamon
¼ teaspoon ground ginger
⅛ teaspoon ground cloves
½ package (2.8-ounce size) whipped topping mix (1 envelope)
Skim milk
¼ cup graham cracker crumbs

Sprinkle gelatin on apple juice in 1-quart saucepan to soften; add water. Heat over low heat until gelatin is dissolved, stirring constantly; remove from heat. Mix pumpkin, brown sugar, cinnamon, ginger and cloves in medium bowl; stir in gelatin mixture until smooth. Refrigerate until mixture mounds slightly when dropped from a spoon, stirring occasionally.

Prepare topping mix as directed on package—except use skim milk. Reserve ½ cup topping. Beat pumpkin mixture until smooth and light; fold remaining topping into pumpkin mixture. Sprinkle crumbs in bottom of square pan, 9 × 9 × 2 inches, sprayed with nonstick cooking spray; spread pumpkin mixture in pan. Cover and refrigerate until firm, at least 2 hours. Top with remaining topping. **9 squares**

PER SQUARE WITH 1 TABLESPOON TOPPING: Calories 85; Protein 2 g; Carbohydrate 17 g; Fat 1 g; Cholestrol 0 mg; Sodium 20 mg

Frosted Banana Bars

⅔ cup sugar
½ cup low-fat sour cream
2 tablespoons margarine, softened
2 egg whites or ¼ cup cholesterol-free egg product
¾ cup mashed very ripe bananas (about 2 medium)
1 teaspoon vanilla
1 cup all-purpose flour
¼ teaspoon salt
½ teaspoon baking soda
2 tablespoons finely chopped walnuts
Frosting (below)

Heat oven to 375°. Spray square pan, 9 × 9 × 2 inches, with nonstick cooking spray. Beat sugar, sour cream, margarine and egg whites in large bowl on low speed 1 minute, scraping bowl occasionally. Beat in bananas and vanilla on low speed 30 seconds. Beat in flour, salt and baking soda on medium speed 1 minute, scraping bowl occasionally. Stir in nuts. Spread in pan.

Bake 20 to 25 minutes or until light brown; cool. Spread with Frosting. Cut into 2¼ × 1½-inch bars. **24 bars**

PER BAR: Calories 90; Protein 1 g; Carbohydrate 18 g; Fat 2 g; Cholesterol 2 mg; Sodium 70 mg

Frosting

1¼ cups powdered sugar
1 tablespoon margarine, softened
1 to 2 tablespoons skim milk
½ teaspoon vanilla

Mix all ingredients until smooth.

Apricot-Meringue Squares and Frosted Banana Bars (page 77)

Apricot-Meringue Squares

Any flavor of jam is delicious in this recipe. To make cutting the dessert into squares easier, simply wet the knife to keep it from sticking.

1 cup all-purpose flour
¼ cup powdered sugar
¼ cup margarine, softened
1 egg white
2 egg whites
½ cup granulated sugar
½ cup apricot jam
3 tablespoons miniature semisweet chocolate chips

Heat oven to 350°. Spray square pan, 9 × 9 × 2 inches, with nonstick cooking spray. Mix flour, powdered sugar, margarine and 1 egg white. Press in pan. Bake about 15 minutes or until set.

Increase oven temperature to 400°. Beat 2 egg whites until foamy. Beat in granulated sugar, 1 tablespoon at a time. Continue beating until stiff and glossy. Spread jam over baked layer. Sprinkle with chocolate chips. Spread meringue over jam and chocolate chips. Bake about 10 minutes or until meringue is brown. Cool completely. Cut into 1½-inch squares.   **25 squares**

PER SQUARE: Calories 80; Protein 1 g; Carbohydrate 14 g; Fat 2 g; Cholesterol 0 mg; Sodium 30 mg

Healthy Hints for Low-Calorie Eating

- A small, healthy snack between regular meals can help curb your appetite. Try plain, hot-air-popped popcorn. It's only 30 calories per cup!
- Rice or corn cakes help fill you up, weighing in at around 30 calories each. Try them instead of bread for an open-face "sandwich."
- For a refreshing treat, freeze melon pieces, banana slices or seedless grapes, and eat them anytime the need for a frozen confection strikes.
- Add sparkling water or club soda to fruit juice to cut calories, but keep great taste.
- Mix fresh or frozen unsweetened berries with skim milk in the blender for a filling shake.

Chocolate-Chip Cookies

This cookie uses half the fat and half the chips of ordinary recipes, but you won't miss them. Miniature chocolate chips give the illusion of more chocolate because they distribute so well.

½ cup granulated sugar
¼ cup packed brown sugar
¼ cup margarine, softened
1 teaspoon vanilla
1 egg white or 2 tablespoons cholesterol-free egg product
1 cup all-purpose flour
½ teaspoon baking soda
¼ teaspoon salt
½ cup miniature semisweet chocolate chips

Heat oven to 375°. Mix sugars, margarine, vanilla and egg white in large bowl. Stir in flour, baking soda and salt. Stir in chocolate chips. Drop dough by rounded teaspoonfuls about 2 inches apart onto ungreased cookie sheet. Bake 8 to 10 minutes or until golden brown. Cool slightly; remove from cookie sheet.

About 2½ dozen cookies

PER COOKIE: Calories 75; Protein 1 g; Carbohydrate 14 g; Fat 2 g; Cholesterol 0 mg; Sodium 65 mg

Cocoa-Oatmeal Cookies

The dough may seem too liquid at first, but the oats and cocoa will absorb the excess moisture. Carob chips may be substituted in this recipe. They have a sweet, distinctive flavor. To make them "go farther," you can chop them up a bit.

1½ cups sugar
½ cup margarine, softened
½ cup plain nonfat yogurt
¼ cup water
1 teaspoon vanilla
½ teaspoon chocolate extract, if desired
2 egg whites or ¼ cup cholesterol-free egg product
3 cups quick-cooking oats
1¼ cups all-purpose flour
½ cup miniature semisweet chocolate chips*
⅓ cup cocoa
½ teaspoon baking soda
¼ teaspoon salt

Heat oven to 350°. Mix sugar, margarine, yogurt, water, vanilla, chocolate extract and egg whites in large bowl. Stir in remaining ingredients. Drop dough by rounded teaspoonfuls about 2 inches apart onto ungreased cookie sheet. Bake 9 to 11 minutes or until almost no indentation remains when touched.

About 5½ dozen cookies

PER COOKIE: Calories 45; Protein 1 g; Carbohydrate 7 g; Fat 2 g; Cholesterol 0 mg; Sodium 50 mg

½ cup carob chips can be substituted for the chocolate chips.

Chocolate-Chip Cookies and Cocoa-Oatmeal Cookies

Rice Pudding

A light sifting of cinnamon enhances the top of the microwaved version.

2 egg whites
1 egg
2 cups cooked rice
½ cup sugar
½ cup golden raisins
2 cups skim milk
½ teaspoon vanilla
¼ teaspoon ground cardamom

Heat oven to 325°. Beat egg whites and egg in ungreased 1½-quart casserole. Stir in remaining ingredients. Bake uncovered 50 to 60 minutes, stirring after 30 minutes, until knife inserted halfway between center and edge comes out clean. Serve warm or cold. Immediately refrigerate any remaining pudding. **8 servings**

PER SERVING: Calories 170; Protein 5 g; Carbohydrate 36 g; Fat 1 g; Cholesterol 30 mg; Sodium 245 mg

MICROWAVE DIRECTIONS: Prepare as directed—except use 1½-quart microwavable casserole and decrease skim milk to 1½ cups. Elevate casserole on inverted microwavable pie plate in microwave oven. Microwave uncovered on medium (50%) 8 to 10 minutes, stirring every 3 minutes, just until creamy. (Pudding will continue to cook while standing.) Let stand uncovered on heatproof surface 10 minutes. Sprinkle with ground cinnamon if desired. Cover and refrigerate any remaining pudding.

Brownies

These cocoa brownies have ⅓ fewer calories than our traditional cocoa brownies. Brownies made with unsweetened baking chocolate may have up to 300 calories each.

⅔ cup packed brown sugar
⅓ cup reduced-calorie margarine, melted
1 teaspoon vanilla
1 egg
1 egg white
⅔ cup all-purpose flour
⅓ cup cocoa
⅓ cup chopped walnuts
½ teaspoon baking powder
½ teaspoon salt
Powdered sugar

Heat oven to 325°. Spray square pan, 8 × 8 × 2 inches, with nonstick cooking spray. Mix brown sugar, margarine, vanilla, egg and egg white. Stir in remaining ingredients except powdered sugar. Spread in pan.

Bake until wooden pick inserted in center comes out clean, about 20 minutes; cool. Cut into 2-inch squares; sprinkle with powdered sugar. Store tightly covered. **16 brownies**

PER BROWNIE: Calories 105; Protein 1 g; Carbohydrate 14 g; Fat 5 g; Cholesterol 15 mg; Sodium 130 mg

Chocolate Swirl Cheesecake

It takes about 12 hours to prepare Thick Yogurt for this recipe. One taste of this scrumptious, low-calorie dessert will convince you that the extra time was worth it!

Thick Yogurt (right)
4 chocolate wafers, crushed (about ¼ cup)
1 package (8 ounces) Neufchâtel cheese, softened
⅔ cup sugar
¼ cup skim milk
2 tablespoons all-purpose flour
2 teaspoons vanilla
3 egg whites or ½ cup cholesterol-free egg product
1 tablespoon cocoa
1 teaspoon chocolate extract
Raspberry Topping (right)

Prepare Thick Yogurt. Heat oven to 300°. Spray springform pan, 9 × 3 inches, with nonstick cooking spray. Sprinkle chocolate wafer crumbs on bottom of pan. Beat Thick Yogurt and cheese in medium bowl on medium speed until smooth. Add sugar, milk, flour, vanilla and egg whites. Beat on medium speed about 2 minutes or until smooth.

Place 1 cup batter in small bowl. Beat in cocoa and chocolate extract until blended. Carefully spread vanilla batter over crumbs in pan. Drop chocolate batter by spoonfuls onto vanilla batter.

Swirl through the batter with metal spatula for marbled effect, being careful not to touch bottom.

Bake 1 hour. Turn off oven; leave cheesecake in oven 30 minutes. Remove from oven; cool 15 minutes. Cover and refrigerate at least 3 hours. Loosen cheesecake from side of pan; remove side of pan. Carefully slide cheesecake onto serving plate if desired. Prepare Raspberry Topping; serve with cheesecake.   **12 servings**

PER SLICE: Calories 190; Protein 6 g; Carbohydrate 30 g; Fat 5 g; Cholesterol 15 mg; Sodium 150 mg

---

THICK YOGURT: Line 6-inch strainer with basket-style paper coffee filter or double-thickness cheesecloth. Place strainer over a large bowl. Spoon 4 cups plain nonfat yogurt into strainer. Cover strainer and bowl and refrigerate at least 12 hours, draining liquid from bowl occasionally.

Rasberry Topping

1 package (10 ounces) frozen raspberries, thawed, drained and juice reserved
¼ cup sugar
2 tablespoons cornstarch

Add enough water to reserved juice to measure 1¼ cups. Mix sugar and cornstarch in 1½-quart saucepan. Stir in juice mixture and raspberries. Heat to boiling over medium heat, stirring frequently. Boil and stir 1 minute; cool.

METRIC CONVERSION GUIDE

U.S. UNITS	CANADIAN METRIC	AUSTRALIAN METRIC
Volume		
1/4 teaspoon	1 mL	1 ml
1/2 teaspoon	2 mL	2 ml
1 teaspoon	5 mL	5 ml
1 tablespoon	15 mL	20 ml
1/4 cup	50 mL	60 ml
1/3 cup	75 mL	80 ml
1/2 cup	125 mL	125 ml
2/3 cup	150 mL	170 ml
3/4 cup	175 mL	190 ml
1 cup	250 mL	250 ml
1 quart	1 liter	1 liter
1 1/2 quarts	1.5 liter	1.5 liter
2 quarts	2 liters	2 liters
2 1/2 quarts	2.5 liters	2.5 liters
3 quarts	3 liters	3 liters
4 quarts	4 liters	4 liters
Weight		
1 ounce	30 grams	30 grams
2 ounces	55 grams	60 grams
3 ounces	85 grams	90 grams
4 ounces (1/4 pound)	115 grams	125 grams
8 ounces (1/2 pound)	225 grams	225 grams
16 ounces (1 pound)	455 grams	500 grams
1 pound	455 grams	1/2 kilogram

Measurements		**Temperatures**	
Inches	Centimeters	Fahrenheit	Celsius
1	2.5	32°	0°
2	5.0	212°	100°
3	7.5	250°	120°
4	10.0	275°	140°
5	12.5	300°	150°
6	15.0	325°	160°
7	17.5	350°	180°
8	20.5	375°	190°
9	23.0	400°	200°
10	25.5	425°	220°
11	28.0	450°	230°
12	30.5	475°	240°
13	33.0	500°	260°
14	35.5		
15	38.0		

NOTE

The recipes in this cookbook have not been developed or tested using metric measures. When converting recipes to metric, some variations in quality may be noted.

Index